T0328201

# Cambridge Elements ≡

Cambridge Elements in International Economics
edited by
Kenneth A. Reinert
*George Mason University*

# THE EAST ASIAN ELECTRONICS SECTOR

## The Roles of Exchange Rates, Technology Transfer, and Global Value Chains

Willem Thorbecke
*Research Institute of Economy, Trade and Industry*

**CAMBRIDGE**
UNIVERSITY PRESS

# CAMBRIDGE
## UNIVERSITY PRESS

Shaftesbury Road, Cambridge CB2 8EA, United Kingdom

One Liberty Plaza, 20th Floor, New York, NY 10006, USA

477 Williamstown Road, Port Melbourne, VIC 3207, Australia

314–321, 3rd Floor, Plot 3, Splendor Forum, Jasola District Centre, New Delhi – 110025, India

103 Penang Road, #05–06/07, Visioncrest Commercial, Singapore 238467

Cambridge University Press is part of Cambridge University Press & Assessment, a department of the University of Cambridge.

We share the University's mission to contribute to society through the pursuit of education, learning and research at the highest international levels of excellence.

www.cambridge.org
Information on this title: www.cambridge.org/9781009216814
DOI: 10.1017/9781009216838

First published 2023

*A catalogue record for this publication is available from the British Library.*

ISBN 978-1-009-21681-4 Paperback
ISSN 2753-9326 (online)
ISSN 2753-9318 (print)

Cambridge University Press & Assessment has no responsibility for the persistence or accuracy of URLs for external or third-party internet websites referred to in this publication and does not guarantee that any content on such websites is, or will remain, accurate or appropriate.

# The East Asian Electronics Sector

## The Roles of Exchange Rates, Technology Transfer, and Global Value Chains

Cambridge Elements in International Economics

DOI: 10.1017/9781009216838
First published online: January 2023

Willem Thorbecke
*Research Institute of Economy, Trade and Industry*
Author for correspondence: Willem Thorbecke, Willem-thorbecke@rieti.go.jp

**Abstract:** The lion's share of smartphones, computers, televisions, semiconductor devices, and other electronic goods is made in East Asia. Final electronic goods are assembled in China and sophisticated parts and components (P&C) such as semiconductor chips, image sensors, and ceramic filters are produced in upstream Asian economies such as Japan, South Korea, and Taiwan. How did Asia become the center of electronics manufacturing? How did Asian workers learn to produce cutting-edge products? Are there lessons for countries like the United States that seek to reshore manufacturing of semiconductors, flat-panel displays, and related products? This Element addresses these issues.

Keywords: East Asia, electronics industry, exchange rates, global value chains, technology transfer

ISBNs: 9781009216814 (PB), 9781009216838 (OC)
ISSNs: 2753-9326 (online), 2753-9318 (print)

# Contents

# 1 Introduction

"Technology adoption and adaptation . . . is really the secret of growth." Ricardo Hausmann (2021)

The lion's share of smartphones, computers, televisions, semiconductor devices, and other electronic goods is made in East Asia. Final electronic goods (FEGs) are assembled in China, and sophisticated parts and components (P&C) such as semiconductor chips, image sensors, and ceramic filters are produced in upstream Asian economies such as Japan, South Korea, and Taiwan. How did Asia become the center of electronics manufacturing? How did Asian workers learn to produce cutting-edge products? Are there lessons for countries like the United States that seek to reshore manufacturing of semiconductors, flat-panel displays, and related products? This Element addresses these issues.

Scholars after World War II expressed pessimism that developing countries could grow through exporting. For instance, Nurkse (1953, 1959) argued that the income elasticity of demand for primary products in developed countries is low. This implies that the ability of developing countries to export more non-manufactured goods to developed countries is limited. Many developing economies therefore chose instead to advance their nascent manufacturing sectors by protecting them from import competition.

East Asian countries, however, turned away from this import substitution strategy and promoted exports. The following sections document these changes and how they contributed to learning and technological progress. One reason exporting proved successful is that the larger market size provided firms with an incentive to innovate (see Akcigit and Melitz, 2021). According to the theory of endogenous growth, the resulting development of new ideas can sustain economic growth (Romer, 1990). High growth rates in the region over several decades persuaded many that export promotion strategies dominate import substitution strategies (see, e.g., Bhagwati, 1988).

Keller (2021) reviewed many studies indicating that trade can generate positive knowledge spillovers. For instance, Acharya and Keller (2009) found that imports into six Organisation for Economic Co-operation and Development (OECD) countries generated research and development (R&D) spillovers that increased total factor productivity. Van Biesebroeck (2005) reported that starting to export increased the productivity of firms across nine African countries by an average of 25%. De Loecker (2007) discovered that Slovenian manufacturing firms that began exporting became more productive than other firms. Garcia-Marin and Voigtländer (2019) documented that Chilean plants that started exporting became 15–25% more productive than non-exporters. Summarizing these and other findings, Keller stated that:

[T]here is by now solid evidence for spillovers through learning-by-exporting that increase firm productivity. Where we know still relatively little is what mechanisms are most important for the spillovers to materialize. The relative contribution of learning about new products or inputs, management techniques, information about new process technologies, or simply demonstration effects is still largely undetermined. (9)

This Element examines these issues by going beyond econometric estimation. It employs a narrative approach to investigate how learning and technological progress occurred in East Asia's flagship electronics industry after World War II.

## Conceptual Background

How did Asian firms and workers acquire the know-how and skills to produce sophisticated electronic goods?[1] Hausmann (2013) noted that much knowledge about production cannot be gleaned from books but is instead tacit and stored in workers' brains. Obtaining this knowledge is difficult, especially for industries that do not exist in a country. Researchers have found that latent knowledge often grows glacially and accumulates through worker migration. Hausmann and Neffke (2019), for instance, reported that, after German reunification, pioneer industries in the east hired workers from the west who possessed the requisite skills and experience. Hausmann also observed that latent knowledge grows through learning-by-doing.

Yoshitomi (2003) provided a framework for understanding how learning and technological progress occur in East Asia. He emphasized that initial conditions such as high saving rates, prudent fiscal policies, low inflation, and flexible labor markets facilitate capital formation. Since knowledge and technology are often imbedded in imported capital goods (see, e.g., Kim and Dahlman, 1992; Lee and Wie, 2015), favorable initial conditions that facilitate capital deepening contribute to learning.

In addition, the quality and technical capabilities of local workers matter. Ohkawa and others noted that workers' technical competence affects their ability to absorb new technologies (Ohkawa and Kohama, 1989; Ohkawa and Rosovsky, 1973). Kiyota and colleagues (2008) found that the intra-firm transfer of managerial technology from foreign affiliates to indigenous workers in China is expedited when workers in the host country are better educated.

Kim (1980), Kim and Dahlman (1992), Yoshitomi (2003), and others differentiated between technology transfer at different stages of development.

---

[1] This section draws on Yoshitomi (2003).

Initially, technologies are imported as a whole. Turnkey plants, foreign machinery, foreign direct investment (FDI), and licensed technology are examples of this. Local firms only assemble foreign P&C. Foreign suppliers provide technical assistance and advice with engineering and managerial issues. They benefit if the technology works and, in the case of original equipment manufacturers (OEMs), they need to ensure that the goods meet high quality standards. As Kim noted, little engineering skill in the host country is required at this stage.

In the second stage domestic workers acquire production experience. This allows them to assimilate new technologies. Countries with more educated workforces can master new technologies more quickly. Firms also engage in R&D and reverse engineering and make limited innovations. Yoshitomi (2003) labeled the R&D at this stage learning, doing, using, and failing (LDUF) in order to distinguish it from cutting-edge research performed at premier universities. Public research institutes can help firms learn new technologies at this stage.

Kim (1980) noted that, as firms face competition in foreign markets, their incentive to improve their technologies increases. Exporting thus helps firms acquire technological prowess. It forces firms to meet high standards set by foreign customers. It also provides access to vast markets, enabling firms to produce in large quantities and to benefit from the learning curve.

In the next stage domestic firms aim to master technologies. They can accomplish this not only by learning-by-doing but also by recruiting skilled workers from abroad and by sending engineers to study at foreign or domestic universities and research institutes. Once a critical mass accumulates of workers with know-how, the workers then migrate from firm to firm and bring their human capital with them. As Yoshitomi (2003) observed, this leads to learning externalities and a virtuous cycle of growth.

At this stage the interests of domestic firms diverge from those of foreign suppliers. Importers seek to leverage technologies while exporters seek to maintain control. Gains can still be made from trade between foreign suppliers and domestic firms if factor endowments differ in the two countries. For instance, if the host country has lower labor costs, home country firms may supply sophisticated capital goods and P&C that host country workers use to assemble final goods. Provided that home country firms can prevent unwanted technology transfers, assembling final goods in the host country benefits them by lowering their production costs.

In the final stage domestic firms approach the technological frontier. They are now in direct competition with technology-supplying firms. At this stage technology transfers are usually effected through strategic alliances.

Yoshitomi (2003) noted that entrepreneurs are the catalyst for technological change. They engage in LDUF and take risks with no guarantee of success. By innovating, they postpone the diminishing returns that set in if more capital is added using the same production techniques. As Hausmann and Rodrik (2003) showed, entrepreneurs also engage in cost discovery. The pioneers learn what goods can be profitably produced in a country given its factor endowment and institutional environment. They then provide external benefits to other entrepreneurs who imitate profitable projects. To the extent that the "flying geese" pattern discussed by Akamatsu (1962) exists in Asia, with advanced countries moving into more advanced industries and less advanced countries moving into the industries abandoned by the more advanced countries, entrepreneurs in the lead countries provide examples for entrepreneurs in follower countries.

## Slicing Up the Value Chain

Entrepreneurs and multinational corporations (MNCs) in Asia have reduced costs and increased productivity by slicing production into fragmented blocks. These value chains include intra-firm trade, arm's-length transactions, and outsourcing (Kimura and Ando, 2005). Production blocks are allocated across the region based on wage levels, factor endowments, technology transferability, physical and human infrastructure, and market-supportive institutions and political regimes in different locations.

Jones and Kierzkowski (1990) modeled the development of cross-border value chains. In their framework firms decide to fragment production when the production cost saving due to fragmentation exceeds the service cost of linking geographically separated production blocks. Their theory implies that lowering the service link cost (SLC) increases production sharing in Asia.

The SLC varies across two dimensions, managerial controllability and geographical distance (Kimura and Ando, 2005). On the controllability dimension, the SLC depends on factors such as the costs of imperfect information, unstable contracts, and uncredible partners.

On the distance dimension, the SLC depends on factors such as the costs associated with transportation, telecommunications, and intra-firm coordination. This framework implies that countries with rampant corruption will face higher controllability costs and thus greater difficulties attracting FDI. On the other hand, regions with high-quality highways, ports, airports, and infrastructure will face lower costs associated with distance and should attract more FDI. As many firms locate in one area, the SLC will fall because it becomes easier to obtain P&C and to handle changes in customer demand when many potential partners are nearby.

## Foreign Direct Investment

How can we understand FDI in East Asia?[2] Mundell (1957) modeled the flow of capital from a capital-abundant country to a capital-scarce country. He showed that, when the capital-scarce country impedes the flow of goods, the capital-abundant country will send capital in search of higher returns. This inflow causes production in the receiving country to shift toward the capital-intensive industry and away from the less capital-intensive industry. The capital flow causes the opposite to happen in the capital-sending country. The disadvantaged industries in both countries thus expand relative to the advantaged industries. The pattern of comparative advantage between the two countries thus changes. The capital flows continue until the difference in comparative advantage and thus the rationale for trade is eliminated. Foreign direct investment in Mundell's model is thus a substitute for trade. This framework implies, consistent with the Rybczynski theorem, that capital inflows cause the capital-intensive industry to expand and the labor-intensive industry to contract.

Kojima (1973), on the other hand, modeled trade and FDI as complements. He posited that FDI flows from the capital-abundant country's disadvantaged industry into the capital-scarce country's advantaged industry. Kojima addressed activities that increase value in industries where the host country is advantaged relative to the home country. As wages increase in the home country and as the capital and knowledge intensity of its output increases, firms transfer labor-intensive production to lower-wage countries. These firms then export sophisticated P&C and capital goods to the downstream country so that there is a complementary relationship between exports and FDI. This framework implies that, contrary to the Rybczynski theorem, capital inflows cause the labor-intensive industry to expand and the capital-intensive industry to contract.

Kojima (1973) represented FDI as a vehicle for transplanting superior production technology to lesser-developed countries through the training of workers and managers. He viewed FDI as transmitting capital, managerial skill, and technical knowledge to the host economy. It transfers know-how and industrial experience concerning techniques for production, material selection and treatment, and machine operation and maintenance. It can include the provision of blueprints and data, the training of engineers and operator, and instruction on factory layout, selection of machinery and equipment, quality and cost controls, and inventory management. As is demonstrated in what follows, much FDI in East Asia followed the Kojima pattern rather than the Mundell (1957) pattern.

This pattern of FDI is related to the flying geese paradigm proposed by Akamatsu (1962). His model holds that, as the lead goose in East Asia advances

---

[2] The next three paragraphs draw on Ozawa (2007) and Thorbecke and Salike (2014).

from labor-intensive production to capital-intensive production, the next geese in the row move into the labor-intensive industries abandoned by the lead goose. The lead goose then advances to more sophisticated industries, the geese in the second row move into the capital-intensive industries abandoned by the lead goose, and the geese in the third row move into the labor-intensive sectors abandoned by the geese in the second row. In this framework Japan is the lead goose. South Korea, Taiwan, and other newly industrialized economies make up the second row. Indonesia, Malaysia, the Philippines, and Thailand make up the third row, and so on.

Thangavelu and Venkatachalam (2020) highlighted four different effects FDI can exert in the host country. They arise because MNCs engaging in inward FDI often have superior technologies and sales networks compared to domestic firms. The first effect is a competition effect. The second is a demonstration effect. The third operates through labor mobility. The fourth works through exporting.

Through the competition channel, foreign firms can harm domestic firms through business stealing or benefit them by forcing them to innovate and be more efficient (see Aitken and Harrison, 1999; Bloom et al., 2016). Through the demonstration effect, domestic firms learn better commercial practices and adopt superior technologies from observing foreign firms in their country. Through the labor mobility channel, domestic firms can benefit if workers migrate from multinationals to local firms and take their human capital with them. Domestic firms can also be harmed if MNCs lure productive workers away. Through the exporting channel, domestic firms can gain if links to foreign MNCs increase their ability to export.

## *Exchange Rates, Trade Imbalances, and Protectionism*

East Asia has run trade surpluses with the rest of the world. Figure 1 shows the region's trade balance in nonelectronic goods and Figure 2 shows its balance in electronic goods. Electronic goods include consumer electronics, telecommunications equipment, computer equipment, electronic components, precision instruments, clock making, and optics.

Figure 1 shows that Asia's trade in nonelectronic goods has often been balanced. It moved to surplus when imports collapsed after the 1997 Asian Crisis and when oil and commodity prices tumbled in 2015. Figure 2 shows that East Asia has run perennial surpluses with the rest of the world in electronic goods and that these surpluses took a quantum jump upward after China joined the World Trade Organization (WTO) in 2001. Since Figures 1 and 2 use different scales, Figure 3 plots the trade balance in nonelectronic and electronic

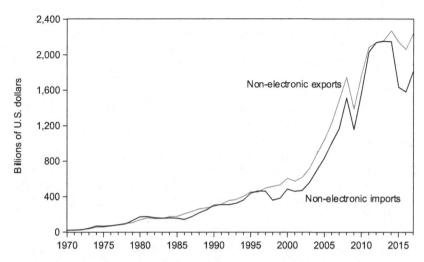

**Figure 1** Nonelectronic exports from East Asia and nonelectronic imports into East Asia

**Notes:** Nonelectronic goods include all goods other than consumer electronics, telecommunications equipment, computer equipment, electronic components, precision instruments, clock making, and optics. East Asia includes China, Japan, Malaysia, the Philippines, Singapore, South Korea, Thailand, and Taiwan. The figure shows exports from East Asian countries to non–East Asian countries and imports into East Asian countries from non–East Asian countries.
**Source:** CEPII-CHELEM database, www.cepii.fr/CEPII/en/bdd_modele/inscription.asp? id=17

goods using the same scale. It shows that East Asia's cumulative surplus since 1980 equaled USD4.36 trillion in nonelectronic goods and $9.44 trillion in electronic goods. Thus 70% of the region's surplus with the rest of the world has been from the electronics industry.

East Asia's surplus with the United States is outsized. Figure 4 shows East Asia's exports to the United States, imports from the United States, and trade balance with the United States. The trade surplus has increased on average by 7% per year from 1985 to 2021. Brief dips during the Global Financial Crisis (GFC) in 2009 and the China–US trade war in 2018 were followed by rapid increases in the surplus. In 2021 East Asia's surplus with the United States equaled USD 650 billion. Using seasonally adjusted data for the first three months of 2022, the surplus is on pace to exceed USD 800 billion in 2022.

The United States has run current account deficits (CAD) continuously since 1982. The CAD rose to 3.1% of gross domestic product (GDP) in 2020 and 3.6% of GDP in 2021 and was forecast to continue growing in 2022.

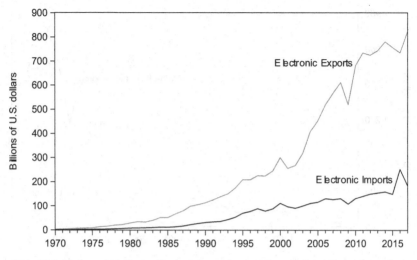

**Figure 2** Electronic exports from East Asia and electronic imports into East
Asia

**Notes:** Electronic goods include consumer electronics, telecommunications equipment,
computer equipment, electronic components, precision instruments, clock making, and
optics. East Asia includes China, Japan, Malaysia, the Philippines, Singapore, South
Korea, Thailand, and Taiwan. The figure shows exports from East Asian countries to
non–East Asian countries and imports into East Asian countries from non–East Asian
countries.
**Source:** CEPII-CHELEM database

The United States can run CAD only if the rest of the world is willing to
finance these by purchasing US assets. If the rest of the world slows its
accumulation of US assets, the US CAD will shrink. As a decrease in the
demand for dollar assets will depreciate the currency, a depreciation of the
US dollar will be part of the current account adjustment.

The effect of a dollar depreciation depends on pricing behavior. If an Asian
exporter responds to the dollar depreciation (Asian currency appreciation) by
keeping the price of their exports in dollars constant (i.e., prices-to-market),
then the volume of their exports to the United States will not fall. Instead, their
revenues in their own currency and thus their profits will fall. If an Asian
exporter responds by raising their dollar export price (i.e., passes through the
exchange rate change), then their volume of exports will fall.

Analyzing data on pass-through, the International Monetary Fund (IMF)
(2007) found that a dollar depreciation would cause some improvement in the
US trade balance. To be effective though, a dollar depreciation needs to be
accompanied by expenditure-reducing policies (e.g., a reduction in the US
budget deficit).

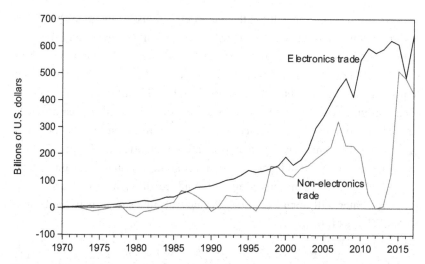

**Figure 3** East Asia's trade balance with the rest of the world in electronic and nonelectronic trade

**Notes:** Electronic goods include consumer electronics, telecommunications equipment, computer equipment, electronic components, precision instruments, clock making, and optics. East Asia includes China, Japan, Malaysia, the Philippines, Singapore, South Korea, Thailand, and Taiwan.
**Source:** CEPII-CHELEM database

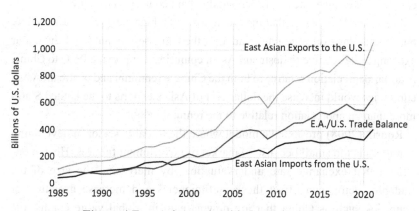

**Figure 4** East Asian trade with the United States
**Notes:** East Asia includes China, Japan, Malaysia, the Philippines, Singapore, South Korea, Thailand, Taiwan, and Vietnam.
**Source:** US Census Bureau

A dollar depreciation against several East Asian currencies would also improve the US trade balance more than a depreciation against a single currency such as the Chinese renminbi. This is because many of America's imports from Asia, especially in the electronics industry, are goods produced within regional value chains. Advanced Asian economies such as Japan, South Korea, and Taiwan export sophisticated P&C to emerging economies such as China and Vietnam. These downstream economies then use labor and capital to produce final goods that are reexported to the United States. For example, Japan provides ceramic filters and image sensors and South Korea provides semiconductors used to produce smartphones in China. Exchange rates throughout the value chain will impact the dollar price of the final goods. Consider the case of advanced Asian economies providing value-added through P&C and China providing value-added through capital and labor. Exchange rates will impact the dollar value of China's exports to the United States, $XV^\$$, as follows:

$$XV^\$ = P_X^\$ \cdot x = \pi^\$ \cdot x + w^{rmb} \cdot L \cdot E^{\$/rmb} + \sum_i Pm^i \cdot m_i \cdot E^{\$/i}, \qquad (1)$$

where $P_X^\$$ is the dollar price of China's exports to the United States, $x$ is the volume of China's exports to the United States, $\pi^\$$ is the Chinese exporter's dollar profit per unit of export, $w$ is the Chinese nominal wage rate measured in renminbi, $L$ is the quantity of labor, $E^{\$/rmb}$ is the Chinese exchange rate (USD per renminbi), $Pm^i$ is the price of imported inputs from supply chain country $i$ measured in the supply chain country's currency, and $E^{\$/i}$ is the supply chain country's exchange rate (USD per supply chain country's currency).[3]

Equation (1) indicates that the dollar costs of China's exports is affected by both the dollar exchange rate relative to the Chinese renminbi and the dollar exchange rate relative to upstream Asian countries that provide P&C to China. A dollar depreciation relative to both the Chinese renminbi and upstream Asian currencies would increase the dollar cost of Asia's exports to the United States more than an appreciation relative to the renminbi alone.

Rodrik (2008) presented a model where the tradable sector in developing countries is too small because of market or government failures. He demonstrated that exchange rate undervaluation, by increasing the size of the tradable sector, can offset these inefficiencies and increase growth. For countries such as China that are downstream in global value chains, the volume of exports and the size of the tradable sector depend, not only on the domestic exchange rate, but also on exchange rates in upstream countries.

---

[3] Equation (1) uses local currency prices for P&C. Lead firms in global value chains typically price the P&C provided by their suppliers in an anchor currency. However, since P&C exporters in countries such as Japan face costs in their local currencies when manufacturing P&C, the local currency prices they receive for their exports remain economically relevant. This is especially true in the longer run as contracts are renegotiated.

Thus undervalued exchange rates in upstream countries may stimulate growth in downstream countries.

Figures 3 and 4 indicate that imbalances between the United States and East Asia increased after China joined the WTO at the end of 2001. How would the resulting trade liberalization affect US labor and capital? In the Heckscher–Ohlin model with two factors and complete factor mobility, the Stolper–Samuelson theorem implies that a decrease in the relative price of the import-competing good (due, for instance, to trade liberalization) would benefit the abundant factor and harm the scarce factor. For the United States, this implies that trade liberalization would increase the return to capital and decrease the return to labor.

Autor, Dorn, and Hanson (2013) found that job losses in the United States following China's WTO accession in 2001 occurred in sectors most exposed to competition from China. Acemoglu and colleagues (2014) and Pierce and Schott (2016) reported that China's imports caused "stunning" losses in US manufacturing jobs. Pierce and Schott noted that many job losses were concentrated in regions such as the southeast, making it harder for workers in the region to find new jobs. Case and Deaton (2015) documented a surge in deaths from suicide, drug abuse, or alcohol-related diseases in middle-aged whites. Pierce and Schott reported that US counties exposed to imports from China experienced more of these "deaths of despair" and that the effects lasted for a long time.[4]

The losses US workers suffered led to protectionist pressure. Concerns that China would dominate key industries and threaten national security, that US firms were being forced to transfer know-how to Chinese firms, and that China was stealing technology multiplied these demands. Protectionist pressures came to a head with the trade war against China initiated by President Trump and continued by President Biden.

## Overview of the Element

Section 2 recounts the rise of Japan's electronics industry after World War II. Entrepreneurs such as Akio Morita at Sony and Tadashi Sasaki at Sharp possessed vision, assumed risks, and competed in demanding consumer markets. Their companies solved cutting-edge scientific problems, harnessed technologies, and ultimately produced world-beating products such as the Sony Trinitron television, the Sony Walkman portable music player, and the Sharp flat-screen television. Japan's rise was aided by high saving rates that provided funds for capital

---

[4] Feenstra and Sasahara (2018) reported that job gains from US exports to the world exceeded job losses from US imports from China.

formation, engineers who received not only technical training but also a liberal arts education, and a global economy tilted toward free trade.

Section 3 investigates how Taiwan and South Korea became leaders in the electronics industry. Taiwanese firms learned to manufacture TVs from Japanese firms and by 1973 Taiwan became the third-leading television exporter. In 1974 the Taiwanese government promoted the integrated circuit (IC) industry and produced world-class firms such as the Taiwan Semiconductor Manufacturing Company. Engineers absorbed technology from RCA in the United States and from Chinese-American scientists and engineers. Many of them returned to work in Taiwan. Clusters with science parks, universities, and firms also emerged. Human capital spread quickly within these networks and generated a virtuous cycle of growth.

Industrial policy faces problems of incentive and knowledge. In 1974, Taiwan confronted a crisis. It was technically at war with the People's Republic of China (PRC), it had severed relations with a key source of technology and capital (Japan), it faced quotas on textile exports because of the Multi Fibre Arrangement, and it suffered a 47% increase in consumer prices from the first oil shock. Taiwanese citizens viewed economic development as imperative for survival and pulled together to promote the IC industry. This helped align the incentives of government officials, entrepreneurs, and workers. World-class Chinese scholars, engineers, and researchers working in the United States volunteered free of charge to help Taiwan develop its IC sector. This provided the requisite knowledge.

Like Taiwan, South Korea used industrial policy to promote electronics. Large companies such as Samsung received loans at below-market interest rates in order to export. To provide incentives, banks rescinded the loans if the companies failed at exporting. To provide knowledge, the Korean government looked to the products that Japan had exported at the same level of development. The government thus endorsed a flying geese pattern for Korean industries. South Korea faced the continual threat of invasion from the north and workers, entrepreneurs, and government officials viewed economic development as crucial for survival. The Korean economy flourished and Samsung ultimately became a more popular consumer electronics brand than Sony.

Section 4 discusses how exchange rate appreciations and wage increases in Japan, South Korea, and Taiwan in the late 1980s caused Northeast Asian MNCs to transfer production to the Association of Southeast Asian Nations (ASEAN). Initially firms in Thailand and Malaysia engaged in assembly. However, spurred by competition, they engaged in process innovation and adopted automation, statistical quality control, and just-in-time management systems. The slicing up of the value chain became intricate, with factories in Malaysia and Thailand sourcing P&C from throughout the region.

Industrial policy failed in Malaysia. Unlike Taiwan and South Korea, Malaysia did not face a national security crisis. It had overcome threats of rural unrest after two decades of strong growth. The government focused on redistributing wealth and firm ownership to indigenous residents (*bumiputera*) rather than to ethnic Chinese and Indian citizens. When making decisions on leadership at semiconductor companies, admissions to college, and grants to electronics firms, the Malaysian government did not favor the most qualified candidates. The emphasis on redistribution also multiplied rent-seeking activities. In this environment, industrial policy failed to achieve structural transformation.

Section 5 documents the rise of China. China took several steps to attract foreign investment. It established special economic zones (SEZs) that offered lower taxes and reduced regulations to foreign firms. Special economic zones in places like the Pearl River and Yangtze River Deltas boasted superb highways, ports, airports, and other infrastructure. China also joined the WTO in 2001, bolstering confidence that it would maintain consistent policies and respect the rule of law.

Foreign direct investment flooded into China after 2001. Multinational corporations that had previously used ASEAN as an assembly platform moved operations to China. Sophisticated electronic P&C flowed from Japan, South Korea, Taiwan, and MNCs operating in ASEAN to China. China used these to assemble FEGs such as computers, cellphones, and consumer electronics. The combination of entrepreneurs like Steve Jobs, competitively priced P&C produced in upstream Asian economies, and low wages and good infrastructure in China proved unbeatable. By 2008, the value of China's FEG exports exceeded the combined value from the next 14 leading FEG exporters.

While the value of China's exports has surged, much of the value-added comes from imported P&C. Thus it is not only the Chinese exchange rate but also exchange rates in upstream countries supplying P&C that matter for the price competitiveness of China's exports.

Section 6 considers the intense competition and cooperation that developed in Asia after the GFC. Much of the competition arose because electronic product had become commoditized and because of modularization. Firms producing commoditized products engage in price wars. To escape these price wars firms seek to differentiate their products. As seen in the cellphone industry, modularization has made this difficult.

The Taiwanese firm MediaTek released free blueprints that allowed Chinese firms with 10 employees and no experience to manufacture phones. Google made the Android operating system for smartphones available for free. Japanese firms, skilled at craftsmanship and *monotsukuri* (making things), suffered in this digital, software-driven ecosystem where start-ups could mix and match modules to assemble cellphones.

Section 6 also recounts the trade war that the Trump administration lost. In spite of high tariffs against Chinese products, it did not reduce America's aggregate trade deficit. Firms shifted production from China to Vietnam and other places. Since the trade deficit reflects the balance between saving and investment, expenditure-switching policies such as tariffs are unlikely to be effective unless they are accompanied by expenditure-reducing policies such as reductions in the US budget deficit.

The United States is also trying to reshore manufacturing. Subsidies to draw liquid crystal display (LCD) manufacturing from China to Wisconsin failed spectacularly. Attempts to subsidize Intel's production, where CEO Pat Gelsinger earned $179 million in 2021 despite poor stock market performance, are unlikely to produce a vibrant semiconductor industry in the United States. Section 7 considers lessons from the East Asian electronics industry that the United States should follow if it wants to strengthen electronics manufacturing.

## 2 Out of the Ashes

In Japanese legend the Ho-Oo bird descends in peaceful and prosperous times.[5] After World War II few could imagine it was about to land in Japan. The country had lost 3 million people; Tokyo, Nagoya, Kobe, and other cities had been burned; and 25% of the nation's tangible wealth had been destroyed. Americans occupied the country and were reluctant to let Japan rebuild heavy industries. Food was scarce and people feared starvation.

Then, in a break for Japan, the nation became a key supplier of textiles, automobiles, metals, chemicals, helmets, and other goods to United Nations troops fighting in the Korean War. The United States prioritized strengthening Japan to stop the spread of communism.

Saburo Okita and Yonosuke Goto worked with the Ministry of Foreign Affairs to devise a blueprint for Japan's economic recovery (Ohno, 2017). They emphasized that Japan would lose its advantage in textiles and agriculture to the rest of Asia and should develop skilled labor–intensive products. They highlighted the need for industrialization and technological improvement. Increasing productivity in this way gained urgency as the Korean War created

---

[5] This section draws on the excellent book by Johnstone (1999).

inflation. When combined with Japan's fixed nominal exchange rate, inflation caused Japan's real exchange rate to be overvalued and its exporters to lose price competitiveness (Ohno, 2017).

To raise productivity, Japan needed to assimilate new technologies. The United States encouraged Japanese scientists and engineers to visit US laboratories and factories to learn. When they returned to Japan they pursued research and development to build on what they had gleaned. Since they were forbidden from making military goods, they focused on consumer products.

America's Bell Labs invented the transistor in 1946. Within three months the Japanese government–sponsored Electro-Technical Laboratory assembled a group led by Makoto Kikuchi to study transistors. When new issues of *Physics Review*, the *Journal of Applied Physics*, and other scientific publications arrived at the library for US armed forces, these and other researchers would study and copy by hand articles on transistors and related technologies (Johnstone, 1999).

As a result of an antitrust ruling, Bell Labs provided transistor technology to interested companies. Tadashi Sasaki from Kobe Kogyo visited the transistor's inventor at Bell Labs in 1951, learned about the technology, and received geranium that could be used to make transistors. His company then signed a licensing agreement with RCA that gave it access to know-how and in 1953 it became the first Japanese company to mass-produce transistors.

## Sony

In 1953 Akio Morita, cofounder of Tokyo Tsushin Kogyo (Totsuko, later renamed Sony), signed a licensing agreement with Western Electric in the United States to make transistors. The Ministry of International Trade and Industry (MITI), however, was angry that Morita had not consulted MITI and refused to support the agreement. While cofounder Masaru Ibuka appealed MITI's decision, Totsuko formed a study group on transistors headed by Kazuo Iwama. The Ministry relented in 1954, and Iwama embarked on a study tour of US factories and laboratories. As he took copious notes, researchers at Totsuko studied the Bell Labs manual entitled *Transistor Technology*. In 1954 they succeeded in manufacturing their first transistor. This enabled them to compete with larger companies that made radios using vacuum tubes.

Totsuko's first transistor radio, introduced in 1955, was the TR-55. Its dimensions were 5.5 x 3.5 x 1.5 inch (140 x 89 x 38.5 mm). Totsuko engineers then sought to make transistor radios pocket-sized. This was difficult because transistors, condensers, speakers, and other parts had to be miniaturized.

In 1957 Totsuko encountered problems constructing the high-frequency transistors needed to improve its radios. Leona Esaki headed a team from the company to investigate the problem. He found that, contrary to the predictions of classical physics, increasing the voltage to the transistor reduced the current and caused negative resistance. Esaki employed the concept of tunneling from quantum mechanics to solve this puzzle. This not only helped Totsuko to manufacture better radios, but also won Esaki a Nobel Prize in physics.

In December 1957 Totsuko introduced the TR-63 transistor radio. Its dimensions were 4.4 x 2.8 x 1.3 inch (112 x 71 x 32 mm). It could fit in a large pocket. The radio was popular in the United States and consumers bought more than 7 million units. Sharp and Toshiba began producing transistor radios and selling many in the United States. In 1959 Japan exported 6 million radios to the United States. To escape cutthroat competition, Sony produced high-end radios and in 1960 used transistors to manufacture black-and-white TVs.

In 1968 Sony patented a new technology called aperture-grille and used this to make Trinitron color televisions. The picture quality was bright, and Sony was able to charge higher prices for these televisions. Sony's patents protected it for the next 20 years from the strenuous price competition that other television makers faced.

Transistors and semiconductors played an important role in Sony's forays into radios and TVs. In 1973 Iwama, now deputy president, learned that semiconductor research at Sony was dying. One project remained for Sony engineers – the charge-coupled device (CCD). Engineers had learned about the device almost as soon as it was invented in 1969 from reading the *Bell System Journal*. As Johnstone (1999) recounted, many Japanese researchers immediately visited Bell Labs and the CCD inventors freely shared what they knew.

The CCD had the potential to revolutionize the video camera. Iwama directed his researchers to focus on CCD development. According to lead researcher Shigeyuki Ochi, engineers were free to research and play around with CCDs.[6] The problem with this technology was that images generated using these devices were covered with white spots. Makoto Kikuchi, now the research director at Sony, remembered from his research at the Electro-Technical Laboratory that spots could come from metal impurities on silicon crystals. The engineers solved this and other problems and transferred CCD production to the factory floor. In 1985 Sony marketed an 8 mm camcorder incorporating CCD technology. The camcorder became one of Sony's most profitable products.

Morita and Ibuka suggested to their engineers and designers at Sony that a portable cassette player would be popular with consumers. The employees

---

[6] Johnstone (1999), p. 186.

produced the Sony Walkman, a cassette player weighing between 10 and 14 ounces (300–400 grams). They also designed headphones that weighed less than 2 ounces (50 grams). The sound quality was good and after introducing the Walkman in 1979, Sony sold more than 400 million units.

## Seiko

Seiko opened business as a clock maker in Tokyo in the nineteenth century and produced its first mechanical watches in 1924. In the 1950s Seiko was Japan's leading watchmaker. In 1960 it produced the Grand Seiko, seeking to release the world's most accurate watch. However, in 1960 an American watch company, Bulova, produced an electronic watch called the Accutron that employed a 360 Hertz tuning fork as its timekeeping device instead of the traditional balance wheel. It was accurate to within one minute per month, far better than the mechanical watches that Seiko and other companies manufactured.

Seiko assembled a team of engineers to study how to make its watches more accurate. The team identified quartz as a material that oscillates at a high frequency when electric voltage is applied. It initiated a project to use quartz to make accurate timepieces.

In 1959 Seiko president Shoji Hattori decided to pursue making Seiko the official timekeeper for the 1964 Tokyo Olympics.[7] He sent managers to observe the 1960 Olympics and instructed his companies to construct chronographs, clocks, and printers. These soon met international standards and Seiko became the timekeeper. It made a quartz stopwatch that recorded times to the hundredths of a second and a printer that printed out times immediately after a race. In the woman's 80 meter hurdles final, three women finished with a time of 10.5 seconds and race officials could not determine who had won. Seiko's timer indicated that one woman had a time of 10.54, the second a time of 10.55, and the third a time of 10.56. Olympic officials were thus able to determine who would receive the gold, silver, and bronze medals. This was the first time that the Olympics had recorded times to hundredths of a second.

In 1969 Seiko produced its first quartz watch, the Astron. It was accurate to within one minute per year, an order of magnitude better than the Bulova Accutron. However, the parts used to construct the Astron were complex and the organization haphazard. Each watch cost 450,000 yen, as much as a car. Seiko abandoned the Astron and pursued quartz watches that would appeal to consumers. To do this, it needed to increase battery life by developing ICs that required little power.

---

[7] The next two paragraphs draw on Tomizawa (2019).

Seiko's research team identified complementary metal oxide semiconductors (C-MOS) as a viable candidate. It could not find a company that would supply C-MOS to them, so Suwa Seiko, one of Seiko's four branches, sought to make them on its own. Unfortunately Suwa Seiko had no experience in semiconductor manufacturing. It sent three engineers to the government's Electro-Technical Laboratory for a year to study how to make semiconductors. The engineers worked day and night to learn the new technology.

Another group company, Dai-ni Seikosha, began receiving ICs from an American company called Intersil. Intersil sent a specialist to Dai-ni Seikosha to teach its employees to manufacture microchips. Suwa Seiko sought help from this expert and by November 1971 it had succeeded in making C-MOS. It used these to manufacture highly accurate, inexpensive quartz watches and also supplied them to other watchmakers. By 1980 these microchips had revolutionized the watch industry.

Seiko also made watches with digital displays. Initially digital displays were made with light-emitting diodes (LEDs). This technology required a lot of power. Seiko then licensed LCD technology from Hoffman-La Roche in Switzerland; LCDs used little power and Seiko began manufacturing LCD digital displays for watches.

One problem with digitalization, as Johnstone (1999) noted, is that a company no longer needed the specialized skills of watchmakers. For hundreds of years craftsmen had refined the art of making mechanical watches with dials and hands. With digital watches, a company that had never made watches could take quartz, LCD displays, and other components and assemble a watch. In the twenty-first century the ability to construct products from components would threaten the Japanese electronics industry.

### Sharp

In 1964 Tadashi Sasaki moved from Kobe Kogyo to Hayakawa Electrical Industries (later renamed Sharp Corporation). Sasaki had studied electrical engineering at Kyoto University in the 1930s. He had then studied at Dresden University in Germany under the renowned professor Heinrich Barkhausen. During World War II he researched vacuum tubes for telephones, radios, and radar. After the war the US army sent him to Western Electric's Pennsylvania factory to study tube manufacturing. While there, he discussed with John Bardeen from Bell Labs how to miniaturize vacuum tubes. Sasaki also worked with Professor Karl Spangenberg from Stanford University on reducing the distance between a cathode that emits negatively charged electrons and the grid (gate) that allows electrons to reach the electrode (Aspray, 1994). In 1946

Bardeen and two colleagues placed the grid into the cathode, inventing the transistor. Sasaki was present on that occasion and realized the magnitude of the breakthrough.

Sasaki believed that the ability to add transistors to an IC could transform consumer electronics. Many companies still used cumbersome vacuum tubes. He thought products could be miniaturized and envisioned a low-cost calculator run on batteries that housewives could carry (Aspray, 1994). His engineers considered this unrealistic. Sasaki sent three of them to Osaka University to study calculator technology anyway (Johnstone, 1999).

In 1966 Hayakawa produced a calculator employing 145 bipolar ICs. Bipolar ICs are problematic, though, because they generate a lot of heat. The company turned to MOS chips. However, Hayakawa could not find a supplier either in Japan or in the United States. Chips for the consumer market had low margins, whereas chips for military use were lucrative. Finally Sasaki convinced an American company, Autonetics, to make MOS chips for calculators. As Johnstone (1999) recounted, Sasaki told the Autonetics CEO that the company could benefit from the learning curve by mass-producing chips. Though profits would be meager in the beginning, they would increase as Autonetics gained experience and increased production yields. Autonetics faced many problems and missed many deadlines manufacturing the chips, but sent the first one to Hayakawa in September 1969.

In October 1969 Hayakawa introduced the Sharp QT-8D calculator. It used four MOS chips each containing 900 transistors. It was the first calculator to use large-scale integration (i.e., more than 500 transistors on a microchip). Its dimension were 9.6 x 5.2 x 2.75 inch (245 x 132 x 70 mm), the smallest calculator available at the time. Within a year, Hayakawa had produced 1 million calculators.

In December 1970 Hayakawa introduced the Sharp EL-8 calculator. This was the first battery-powered portable calculator. Its dimensions were 4 x 6.5 x 2.8 inch (102 x 164 x 70 mm) and its weight with batteries was 1 pound 9 ounces (0.72 kg).

Other Japanese firms imitated Sharp by buying integrated processors from the United States and producing calculators. Japanese chipmakers complained to MITI and MITI no longer permitted Japanese companies to buy US microchips.

As Johnstone (1999) noted, Sharp's first calculators required 10 watts of power. If Sharp could use LCD displays, the electricity required would be three orders of magnitude less. In 1971 Sasaki asked RCA, which held the patents for LCDs, if RCA could produce LCD displays for Sharp calculators. RCA thought that the technology would not be profitable for consumer applications and declined (Aspray, 1994). Instead it licensed the technology to Sharp for

$3 million. RCA invited four researchers from Sharp to visit its laboratories and talk to its experts. Sharp then invested heavily in making its own LCD panels. In 1973 Sharp introduced the first LCD calculator. Billions of calculators have since been sold, and Sharp has been a leading producer. Sasaki highlighted the ability to make its own LCD chips, saying that if Sharp had bought chips from RCA there might no longer be a Sharp Corporation (Aspray, 1994).

After Sharp and Seiko developed LCD technology for calculators and watches, they investigated this technology for televisions. Liquid crystal displays combined with thin film transistors (TFTs) offered the possibility of producing thin televisions that could hang on a wall. Seiko produced the first LCD color TV in 1984. Its screen was only 2 inches, though. In 1987 Sharp built a 3-inch LCD TV. Sharp's research director then instructed his staff to design a 14-inch version. As Johnstone (1999) observed, the engineering challenge was immense. This would require a million TFTs. In 1988 Sharp succeeded in building it and in 1990 this invention won the Eduard Rhein Technology Award, considered the Nobel Prize of the audiovisual world.

Engineers at Sharp and Seiko commended the positive research environments at their companies. Tomio Wada, who pioneered LCD research at Sharp, said that management supported the researchers as they pursued their dreams. Yoshio Yamazaki, who initiated LCD work at Seiko, said that the company placed almost no restrictions on his research.[8]

## The Semiconductor Industry

Sony, Seiko, Sharp, and other companies produced chips to use in their products. Firms that produce semiconductors for their own use are called captive firms. Firms that produce semiconductors for other firms are called merchant firms. Seiko was a merchant firm. Sharp obtained chips from a merchant firm in the United States, Autonetics. Other Japanese firms imitated Sharp by buying ICs from the United States and producing calculators. Japanese chipmakers, who originally refused to produce chips for Sharp to make calculators, appealed to MITI, and MITI no longer allowed Japanese companies to buy US microchips. This would prove to be shortsighted.

Sharp and Seiko had leapfrogged to making C-MOS chips without first learning to make the industry standard P-MOS (positive channel MOS) and N-MOS (negative channel MOS). American semiconductor companies were wedded to P-MOS and then N-MOS chips. Sasaki argued that C-MOS would pose fewer battery problems for calculators if people wanted to use them for a long time. The C-MOS chips required five orders of magnitude less power

---

[8] Wada and Yamazaki's comments are quoted by Johnstone (1999, p. 126).

than bipolar or other MOS ICs. Sasaki also thought that P-MOS was slower for calculations. Thus he pushed for C-MOS chips for calculators (Aspray, 1994). When Toshiba engineers asked Sasaki in 1970 for advice about semiconductors, he insisted that they make C-MOS chips (Johnstone, 1999).

Manufacturing C-MOS chips was more difficult than making P-MOS or N-MOS chips. Japanese firms persevered, though, and by 1980 produced chips that American users recognized as of the highest quality in the world (Okimoto, Sugano, and Weinstein, 1984). Bernard Vonderschmitt, manager of solid-state electronics at RCA, recounted that no American firms saw the potential of C-MOS technology until the late 1970s or early 1980s (Johnstone, 1999). Thus, in the 1980s, when C-MOS became the industry standard, Japanese producers held the upper hand. Japanese companies were also helped by the 65% appreciation of the dollar between 1979 and 1985 that increased their price competitiveness relative to US producers (Irwin, 1996).

No Japanese manufacturer was among the top 10 producers in 1980, but by 1986 Japan had become the world's leading semiconductor supplier. American semiconductor companies had a 60% share of the world market in 1979 and Japanese companies a share of less than 30%. Both nations had 45% of the market in 1985 and after this Japanese firms pulled ahead. In dynamic random access memory (DRAM) semiconductors, the US market share tumbled from 70% in 1978 to 20% in 1986. Meanwhile over these eight years the Japanese share rose from less than 30% to 75% (Irwin, 1996). Japanese semiconductor manufacturers included NEC, Toshiba, Hitachi, Fujitsu, Mitsubishi, and Matsushita.

### Educational, Macroeconomic, and Trade Policy Backdrop

The period from 1950 to the 1980s was the golden age of the Japanese electronics industry. Entrepreneurs took risks, engineers dreamed, factory workers manufactured, and consumers enjoyed pocket-sized radios, Walkmans, camcorders, portable calculators, flat-screen TVs, and many other innovations.

What type of education did Japanese workers receive at this time? Hayami and Goto (2011) found that in 1950 the average years of schooling of the working-age population in Japan was at 70% of the frontier country (the United States) and by 1970 this had increased to 80%. Ikeda and Morita (2019) reported that until 1940 Japanese colleges graduated fewer than 5,000 engineers per year, but this number exceeded 10,000 in 1955, 20,000 in 1960, 30,000 in 1965, and 50,000 in 1970. Sawa (2013) noted that the Japanese engineers active during this era (those educated from before World War II until 1975) received not only technical training but also a broad liberal arts

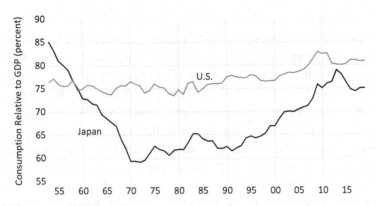

**Figure 5** Consumption relative to GDP for Japan and the United States
**Source:** Penn World Table

education in literature, philosophy, and history. Sawa, echoing Steve Jobs, argued that the combination of technical training and liberal arts contributed to the success of the consumer electronics industry.[9]

Many Japanese consumers had faced extreme poverty during the 1930s and privations during World War II. After the war food was in short supply and many feared starvation. These experiences increased their propensity to save. As the economy prospered after the war, workers saved the increases in income rather than spending them. This is clear in Figure 5, which presents consumption relative to GDP for the frontier country (the United States) and for Japan. For the United States consumption relative to GDP remained constant, whereas for Japan it fell by 25 percentage points between 1953 and 1970. The life-cycle and permanent income theories of consumption indicate that consumption should be a stable multiple of a consumer's long-term income. This held for the United States after World War II, but not for Japan. Japanese households saved rather than spent much of the increase in income. This pool of saving facilitated investment. Figure 6 shows that Japanese capital formation relative to GDP soared between 1960 and 1980 while it remained almost constant for the United States.

The trading environment in Japan's largest market, the United States, was tilted toward free trade for much of this period. After the perceived failure of the Smoot–Hawley Tariff Act in 1930 the United States began liberalizing trade with the Reciprocal Trade Agreements Act in 1934. After World War II the United States dominated the world economy and many American industries

---

[9] When introducing the iPad 2 in March 2011, Jobs said, "Technology alone is not enough – it's technology married with liberal arts, married with the humanities, that yields us the results that make our heart sing" (Carmody, 2011).

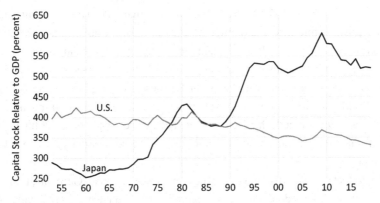

**Figure 6** Capital stock relative to GDP for Japan and the United States
**Source:** Penn World Table

lobbied for open trade. The desire to contain communism also caused the United States to open its markets. In addition the United States had an advantage in high-technology industries, motivating advanced sectors such as electronics to pursue freer trade.

By the 1980s, however, this had changed. The dollar appreciated by 65% between 1979 and 1985 in the wake of contractionary monetary policies by the Federal Reserve and large budget deficits by the Reagan administration. This appreciation damaged the price competitiveness of American firms and led to unprecedented trade deficits. Congress demanded trade protection. Japan, whose trade surplus approached 4% of GDP in 1984, was a target. In 1985, according to Destler (1986), 99 seriously protectionist and 77 potentionally protectionist trade bills were introduced in Congress.

One protectionist episode buffeted the semiconductor industry. As discussed earlier in this Element, between 1979 and 1985 the Japanese semiconductor industry rapidly overtook the US semiconductor industry. Between the first quarter of 1984 and the middle of 1985, the price of a 64 K DRAM fell from $3.00 to $0.75 and the price of a 256 K DRAM fell from $31.00 to $3.00 (Irwin, 1996).

American producers were decimated and sought government relief. American firms filed a Section 301 case against the Japanese government, claiming that they were denied fair access to the Japanese market. One of their complaints was that the Japanese government in the past had overtly excluded US semiconductor firms from the Japanese market. The US government filed an antidumping case against Japanese firms, claiming that Japan was selling chips abroad at less than their fair value. The US government also passed a law in 1984 forbidding copying of US chips.

As the Commerce Department and the International Trade Commission issued positive findings of dumping, the US and Japanese governments reached a negotiated settlement. The settlement hinted strongly that Japan would accede a 20% share of the Japanese semiconductor market to US firms. It also said that the Japanese government would monitor Japanese dumping in third markets. In turn, MITI pressured Japanese firms to raise prices and lower export quantities. As Irwin (1996) noted, the requirement that market share be determined by government fiat rather than by market forces was an extraordinary change in US trade policy.

To deflect protectionist pressures, the United States, Japan, Germany, France, and the United Kingdom agreed in September 1985 to push down the value of the dollar. Between September 1985 and the end of 1987 the yen real effective exchange rate appreciated by 50%. Japanese electronics firms responded by moving factories abroad. This is discussed in Section 4. First, Section 3 turns to the emergence of the electronics industry in South Korea and Taiwan.

## Interpretation

How did Japanese firms acquire the know-how to produce electronic products? They had skilled managers and researchers such as Tadashi Sasaki and Leona Esaki who guided their companies to take intelligent risks. The country at the technology frontier (the United States) freely shared discoveries with Japanese researchers. American firms also licensed technology to Japanese firms and provided experts to impart manufacturing know-how. For instance, experts from an American company, Intersil, enabled Seiko to begin manufacturing C-MOS. Japanese workers were well educated and hardworking, enabling them to assimilate imported technologies.

As Japan's economy recovered, Japanese households saved much of their rising incomes. These funds financed investment by Japanese firms. Firms also channeled profits into R&D and gave engineers freedom to experiment. The number of engineers grew rapidly and they received not only technical training but also a liberal arts education. They were passionate about their research. They were also loyal to their companies. Employment typically lasted for a lifetime. Engineers were eager to achieve breakthroughs for their companies.

Japanese firms could not join the lucrative defense electronics industry, so they focused on consumer electronics. This forced them to continually innovate to escape cutthroat price competition. Public research institutes such as the Electro-Technical Laboratory accumulated and disseminated technical knowledge. For example, in 1947 they spearheaded attempts to understand transistor technology. They also provided a training ground for companies that could not afford to send workers abroad to study. In the late 1960s a team from Seiko studied how to make C-MOS there.

Japanese firms benefited from access to the world's largest consumer market, the United States. They sold millions upon millions of radios, televisions, watches, calculators, and other electronic products to the United States. This led to huge efficiency gains through learning-by-doing.

However, in the early 1980s, as the United States ran large global trade deficits and Japan ran large global surpluses, trade imbalances between Japan and the United States caused protectionist pressures to explode. Almost half of Japan's surplus with the United States at this time was from the electronics industry. To deflect protectionism, Japan agreed in the 1985 Plaza Accord to push down the value of the dollar and in the 1986 Semiconductor Agreement to increase imports into Japan and to raise prices.

## 3 How the Tigers Got Their Claws

The *Oxford English Dictionary* defines a miracle as "a highly improbable or extraordinary event, development, or accomplishment that brings very welcome consequences." The economic transformations of Taiwan and South Korea were miraculous according to this definition. Their economies entered the 1960s dirt poor and ravaged by war. They assimilated technologies, learned new skills, and reached the frontier of the electronics industry. As of 2022 they remained the leading producers of semiconductors and other key electronic goods.

### Taiwan

The Republic of China (ROC), headed by Chiang Kai-Shek, lost the Chinese civil war in 1949 to the People's Republic of China (PRC), headed by Mao Zedong. The ROC evacuated to Taiwan. The ROC and the PRC had armed conflicts in 1954–1955 and 1958. The ROC's GDP per capita in 1960 was below Haiti and Zimbabwe's. Economic development was imperative for Taiwan's survival.

Ta-Chung Liu and Sho-Chieh Tsiang played roles for Taiwan analogous to those Saburo Okita and Yonosuke Goto played in planning Japan's recovery (Bhagwati, 1999; Krueger, 1997). Beginning in 1958 Liu and Tsiang rejected import substitution – the use of protectionist tools to promote industrialization – and advocated encouraging private firms to compete in export markets. To achieve this they convinced the Taiwanese government to abandon overvalued exchange rates, artificially low interest rates, and high tariffs (Yoshitomi, 2003).

Like Japan, Taiwan has limited natural resources and exports can provide foreign exchange to import resources and capital goods. Taiwan also has a small domestic market and needs expansive world markets. Tsiang and Liu high-lighted Taiwan's advantage in labor-intensive exports. Under the export-oriented strategy, the value of Taiwan's textile exports increased 12 times between 1967 and 1974.

Tatung Company initiated transistor radio production in Taiwan in 1961 and by 1962 Taiwan had exported 30,000 units.[10] By 1966 Taiwan had exported 2 million radios, largely for Japanese trading companies (*sogo shosha*) selling to the United States. The *sogo shosha* provided technical assistance to ensure quality control. Tatung, Sampo Corporation, and other Taiwanese companies also began television production in the 1960s, obtaining technology through joint ventures or licensing with Japanese companies. Tatung sent engineers to Japan for training (Hayter and Edgington, 2004). Taiwanese managers, engineers and technicians at other firms also received training, largely from Japanese MNCs (Hobday, 1995b). In addition American and European MNCs used Taiwan as a base from which to assemble and export televisions to the United States. Taiwanese firms assimilated the technologies from MNCs and exported low-cost televisions under their own brand names to developing economies. By 1973 Taiwan was the world's third leading exporter of televisions. Taiwanese firms also learned from MNCs to produce more P&C for televisions and electronic goods. Hobday (1995b) noted that Japanese MNCs sparked a vibrant network of Taiwanese parts and services providers.

In 1974 the Multi Fibre Arrangement was reached and Taiwan faced quotas on textile exports. Taiwan also had to leave the United Nations in 1971 after the United States established diplomatic relations with the PRC. Taiwan severed relations with Japan in 1972 and Japan stopped air transport to Taiwan in 1974. Since Japanese companies were crucial sources of capital goods and technology, this damaged local industries. Taiwan also suffered a 47% increase in consumer prices between 1972 and 1974 due to the first oil shock. In this crisis environment the Taiwanese government focused on industrial upgrading and confidence building.

Taiwan was already investing in education. In 1968 it instituted a nine-year compulsory education system when few countries had nine-year requirements. It later extended this to 12 years.

Taiwanese officials conferred extensively with Chinese experts from the United States. For instance, the ministers of economic affairs and transport met with Wen-yuan Pan in 1974. Pan was a researcher and later director at RCA's prestigious David Sarnoff Laboratories in Princeton, New Jersey. Pan argued that the Taiwanese electronics industry consisted of small firms that

---

[10] This paragraph draws on Chen and Ku (2000).

could not cooperate sufficiently. Unlike Japan and Korea, Taiwan was the land of small and medium-sized enterprises (SMEs). These companies could not afford the expensive R&D and capital formation necessary to move beyond assembly operations into higher-value-added activities in the electronics industry.

## The Integrated Circuit Industry

Pan identified semiconductors as a key product with future potential and inter-industry connections.[11] He submitted a plan for the development of the IC industry in Taiwan in 1974. The government accepted his plan, and in September 1974 it established the Research & Development Center of Electronics Industries (later called Electronics Research & Service Organization [ERSO]) as part of the Industrial Technology Research Institute (ITRI). Pan recruited Chinese engineers working in America to staff the center. Since Taiwan had little experience with semiconductors, he also established the Technical Advisory Committee (TAC) composed of leading Chinese researchers at US universities and firms to guide semiconductor development.

The TAC decided that an older technology would provide a good springboard for learning. This technologies would be available from US firms along with technical documents and requisite machinery. The TAC thus recommended that Taiwan assimilate 7.0 micron C-MOS technology when the frontier technology was 3.0 microns. It also advised that the foreign firms would initially transfer technology and that within four years ERSO would develop technology through indigenous research (Lin and Rasiah, 2014).

Pan recommended that the government spend USD 10 million on the project. Lin and Rasiah (2014) noted that this was an enormous sum when Taiwan's per capita income was only USD 400. Many opposed this plan. Nevertheless the government agreed.

In 1976, Taiwan signed a contract with RCA to obtain 7.0 micron technology. RCA agreed to transfer technology for design, process, manufacturing management, and cost accounting (Chang, Shih, and Hsu, 1994). RCA would even teach ERSO how it built its accounting system (Lin and Rasiah, 2014).

The Electronics Research & Service Organization recruited 40 engineers. Several had PhDs from American universities.[12] After providing instruction, ERSO sent them to America for further training by RCA. When they returned to Taiwan in 1977, they built a pilot IC plant and produced their first microchips.

---

[11] This section draws on Chang, Shih, and Hsu (1994) and Liu (1993).

[12] Lin and Rasiah (2014) listed three with PhDs from Princeton who made vital contributions to the project.

As Lin and Rasiah (2014) noted, the engineers producing the ICs had no sales or marketing experience. One of them recruited a classmate who was a businessman in Hong Kong. With his help, ERSO sold thousands of ICs to electronic watch-makers. Through learning-by-doing, ERSO in 1979 achieved production yields better than those at RCA (Breznitz, 2007).

The Electronics Research & Service Organization then sought to transfer the know-how to private industry. Since no existant companies were capable of absorbing the technology, ERSO created the United Microelectronics Corporation (UMC) in 1979, which joined the Hsinchu Science Based Industrial Park (HSBIP). Minister of Science and Technology Shien-Siu Shu had established HSBIP in 1979. Its director, Dr. Irving Ho, had received 36 US patents while a researcher at IBM in the United States, and HSBIP is located next to two universities, National Tsing Hua University and National Chiao Tung University. Thus UMC was not only close to active researchers but also received low-interest loans, inexpensive land, and tax holidays from HSBIP.

The Electronics Research & Service Organization transferred to UMC a manufacturing supervisor, a testing manager, a sales manager and supervisor, a quality control manager, and a circuit design manager. It also transferred process and product technologies, including technologies to manufacture melody, telephone, timer, memory, and calculator ICs (Chang, Shih, and Hsu, 1994).

Production began at UMC in April 1982; UMC reached the break-even point in November 1982 and sold more than NT$100 million per month beginning in June 1983 (Chang, Shih, and Hsu, 1994). As of 2021 UMC remained a leading chipmaker with USD 16 billion in assets and 20,000 employees.

After succeeding at spinning off UMC, ITRI turned to very-large-scale integration (VLSI) technology, which refers to placing more than 100,000 devices on a chip. The government invested NT$2.9 billion in this project. While ITRI originally acquired 7.0 micron C-MOS technology from RCA, during this project it succeeded with 1.0 micron technology. It upgraded the pilot IC plant to produce VLSI chips.

After mastering these production techniques ITRI employed them to form a new company called the Taiwan Semiconductor Manufacturing Company (TSMC). The government, private investors, and Phillips Corporation all provided capital to TSMC and ITRI transferred 150 employees and rented its VLSI manufacturing plant to TSMC (Chang, Shih, and Hsu, 1994). The company's first chairman, Morris Chang, had received a PhD from Stanford and served as the vice president of Texas Instruments.

A new business model was inaugurated at TSMC (see Lin and Rasiah, 2014). Previously the same company would design and manufacture ICs; TSMC was the first company that manufactured ICs according to other firms' specifications rather than designing them in-house. This is referred to as a pure-play business model. In 2021 it was the largest pure-play semiconductor manufacturer, with USD 134 billion in assets and more than 65,000 employees.

By focusing on the challenging and capital-intensive task of manufacturing ICs, TSMC allowed other companies to focus on the knowledge-intensive task of designing them. As Lin and Rasiah (2014) noted, this offered a tremendous opportunity for companies that were designing ICs.

In the past, as Morris Chang discussed in Patterson (2007), Japanese companies produced semiconductors for companies lacking manufacturing facilities ("fabless" companies). Brooks (2000) noted that Japanese companies often sought intricate knowledge of the products they were manufacturing. Brooks observed that fabless companies were concerned that Japanese manufacturers were seeking technology that they could use to manufacture chips themselves. Van Agtmael (2007) reported that chip designers live in fear that fabricators will purloin their intellectual property. Semiconductor firms thus remained hesitant to outsource manufacturing to Japanese companies.

On the other hand, TSMC was forbidden by charter from designing or manufacturing ICs under its own name. It thus assured customers that it was a partner rather than a competitor (Van Agtmael, 2007). This allowed it, unlike Japanese manufacturers, to acquire the trust of upstream companies. The success of TSMC thus does not follow the flying geese model, where Taiwan imitated steps taken by the lead goose, Japan. Instead it represents an innovation whereby TSMC was able to gain the trust of hundreds of customers and split up the value chain in a way that has proven profitable for both TSMC and its customers.

To exploit the division of labor between fabs and designers, the Taiwanese government trained many in IC design. As Chang, Shih, and Hsu (1994) discussed, Taiwan needed this know-how in the early 1980s. The National Science Council, the Ministry of Education, and ITRI itself encouraged students and professors to obtain computer-aided design training at ITRI. They also provided design tools to universities and a foundry at ITRI where universities could manufacture their designs. Twelve departments at nine universities participated and 150–200 people received training each year.

In 1983 the government started actively encouraging overseas Chinese with experience at world-class firms and research institutes to return to Taiwan. With the opportunity presented by TSMC, many returned to start up or to work for design companies. Lin and Rasiah (2014) noted that Ming-Qiu Wu brought 27 engineers from Silicon Valley in 1989 and founded Macronix. Chang and Tsai (2002) reported that Taiwanese experts from

Silicon Valley also returned to establish designers Etron and Via Tech. The returnees not only brought advanced technologies but also retained communication channels with Silicon Valley. They could call colleagues in the Valley to resolve technical difficulties (see also Lin and Rasiah, 2014). As they interacted with engineers and researchers at HSBIP, ITRI, National Tsing Hua University and National Chiao Tung University, technical knowledge spread across the cluster.

## The Computer Industry

The computer industry received impetus in the late 1970s from Taiwanese gaming companies.[13] Demand for games exploded and firms imported microprocessors from the United States and games from Japan. They reverse engineered the programmable logic arrays inside the Japanese games, redesigned these circuit boards for local needs, and even exported some (Chen and Ku, 2000). In 1980 the Ministry of Education banned video games and local producers needed new uses for the microprocessors they had stockpiled. They employed them to build low-priced Apple clones. The government banned these machines. Electronics firms then licensed technology from IBM and created legal IBM-compatible machines.

Many Taiwanese firms were too small or lacked capital to undertake R&D. The government had prioritized the development of computers and peripherals in 1978 and established the First Computer Project in 1979. The Industrial Technology Research Institute performed R&D for local computer manufacturers. It also sent researchers to Wang Computer Company in Massachusetts for training and technology transfer. As Chang, Hsu, and Tsai (1999) noted, ITRI transferred the Z80 computer CMC-100 technology to Hong-yu Company in 1982 and assisted ACER and four other companies with the technologies to manufacture IBM-compatible PC-XTS AND PC-ATs in 1983 and 1984. In 1985 Acer became the second company in the world to manufacture 32-bit personal computers. An alliance between Apple, IBM Motorola and major Taiwanese computer makers to research Power-PC computers was formed by ERSO (Chen and Ku, 2000).

Taiwanese firms used their expertise in making televisions to manufacture computer monitors. A Tatung subsidiary became the world's largest producer of cathode ray tubes (CRTs) for computer monitors. Tatung, Sampo, and other companies became leading producers of monitors, often as subcontractors for foreign MNCs. Engineers released from the televisions supply chain migrated to the computer supply chain.

---

[13] This section draws on Chen and Ku (2000).

The network of P&C suppliers that had developed to support the television industry turned to producing parts for computers, computer monitors, and other peripherals. The SMEs within these networks became experts in particular niches (Chen and Ku, 2000). They then worked with other small firms in the value chain to produce motherboards, keyboards, and other inputs for final computer systems. Hayter and Edgington (2004) noted that MNCs became dependent on the skill and engineering talent of SMEs within these networks. Hattori and Sato (1997) observed that the flexibility and rapid responses of Taiwan's interwoven SME networks are ideal for the short product cycles and volatile demand in the computer industry.

An example of these networks comes from motherboard producers who use printed circuit boards (PCBs) as inputs. Local firms had experience building PCBs from making televisions, games, and calculators. Designers using this experience or training from ERSO or in the United States sent designs to PCB manufacturers. The PCB fabrication was disaggregated into discrete tasks. One company imprinted the PCBs. Other companies added electronic components. Inserting the components was also divided into subtasks: automatic insertion, surface-mount insertion, and hand insertion. The capital-intensive subtasks could be allocated to one set of firms and the labor-intensive subtasks to another (Chen and Ku, 2000; Kawakami, 1996). Design and PCB manufacturing are at the heart of the motherboard industry. Taiwan soon dominated this industry. The leading circuit board producer in the early 1990s, Taiwan's First International Computer Incorporated, accessed the latest technology by conducting research with Intel, Texas Instruments, Microsoft, and Motorola (Hobday, 1995b).

Research in computer peripherals was sponsored by ITRI and HSBIP. In 1980 Dr. Irving Ho at HSBIP invited Benny Hsu to return from the United States and establish a company. Hsu founded Microtek together with Taiwanese researchers working at Xerox in the United States. Microtek focused on research and designed a device that could debug circuit board designs. Then, with help from ITRI, they manufactured the world's first desktop scanner in 1984 and the first scanner capable of storing images on a computer in 1986. They taught upstream companies how to make the requisite parts. Some workers left and started other scanner manufacturers that surpassed Microtek (Royal, 2004). Taiwan became a world leader in producing scanners and other peripherals such as computer mice, CD-ROM drives, and video cards. Often a small company would master the technology for a narrow product category or occupy a niche market such as scanners for hospitals (Chen and Ku, 2000). They produced many of these goods as subcontractors for famous brands.

Research into and strategies for developing notebook computers were also supported by ITRI. Taiwan introduced notebook personal computers in 1990, the same year advanced countries did. In 1991 it exported 500,000 notebooks and by 1996 it had produced one-third of the world's output of notebooks (Chang, Hsu, and Tsai, 1999). It produced many of these as OEMs for established brands.

Taiwan's overall output of computer products also soared. In 1980 it exported only 0.5% of the world's computer goods. By 1992, this number had increased to 7.1% and Taiwan was tied as the fourth leading exporter of computer equipment.[14]

## South Korea

South Korea's GDP per capita in 1960 was below Haiti and Zimbabwe's. Most of its output came from the primary sector and manufacturing's share was only 15%. Korea depended on US military and humanitarian aid and instability and discontent multiplied. Major General Chung-Hee Park took over in a coup in 1961 and was elected president in 1963. He had been an officer in the Japanese army, and the success of Japan's export-oriented growth after World War II convinced him that Korea should adopt a similar approach. Economic development was imperative to resist the military threat from North Korea. Like Japan and Taiwan, Korea had few natural resources and needed to export in order to import military hardware, resources, and capital goods. Unlike Taiwan, Park prioritized the development of large conglomerates called chaebols.

Park's government took control of the banking system and provided working capital at below-market interest rates to the chaebols. If firms succeeded at exporting, banks continued to provide financing; if not they rescinded the credit (Yoshitomi, 2003). Hausmann and Rodrik (2003) noted that of the 10 largest chaebols in 1965, only 3 remained on the list 10 years later. The conglomerates thus had an incentive to succeed at exporting. Korea also began investing heavily in education, progressing from 25% of the average schooling level of the frontier country (the United States) in 1960 to 75% in 2000 (Hayami and Goto, 2011).

One of the industries that Park's government promoted was consumer electronics.[15] As Sato (1997) noted, the government was trying to follow the industrial progression that Japan had pioneered. The Korean government also banned imports to nurture this infant industry. Kim (1980) reported that entrepreneurs starting in the late 1960s imported packaged technologies to produce black-and-white televisions, stereos, and other goods. Their role was limited to assembling imported P&C, and labor contributed only 5% to the value-added of electronic goods. During the first year, foreign experts were vital to helping firms iron out

---

[14] These data come from the CEPII-CHELEM database.
[15] The next several paragraphs draw on Kim (1980).

production problems. Hobday (1995a) noted that US multinationals imparted little technology to Korean firms. In contrast, Japanese multinationals provided not only P&C and capital goods but also training and know-how.

Kim (1980) also reported that, within seven years (by 1975), many additional producers had emerged who were not dependent on foreign training. Instead, workers at the original firms migrated to new firms and brought their human capital and production experience with them.

The government actively encouraged exports through the Electronics Promotion Law of 1969. Firms thus competed abroad. To increase their competitiveness, exporting firms were exempted from tariffs on imported intermediate goods and from local content requirements. Exported goods were produced with high foreign value-added in partnership with foreign firms (Sato, 1997).

There was also substantial competition among domestic firms in the protected Korean market. Goods for the local market were produced by indigenous firms (Sato, 1997). They needed to assimilate foreign technologies to differentiate their products (e.g., larger versus smaller televisions) and to reduce costs. Kim (1980) found that this assimilation was driven by experienced Korean workers rather than by outside experts. He also reported that the international transfer of technology extended to parts such as vacuum tubes and tuners, so that by 1975 the majority of these were produced within Korea. Electronic goods sold to the domestic market thus had high domestic content (Sato, 1997).

Kim (1980) emphasized that R&D also became important by 1975. Out of 31 consumer electronics firms he surveyed, 21 had separate R&D departments. On average the firms reported more than five product improvements per year. Productivity per worker in the industry increased 2.3 times between 1968 and 1975.

By 1975 imported technology was used to produce new goods. For instance, radio equipment was used to construct electronic quality control devices, communications technology was used to make microwave ovens, single side band transreceivers were used to make broadcasting equipment and radar, and calculator technology was developed to make microprocessors. Kim (1980) attributed the successful innovation to government infant industry protection, entrepreneurs skilled at combining foreign technology with inexpensive labor, and a labor force that was more skilled than expected given Korea's level of development. Kim wrote prophetically in 1980 that Korea might begin to challenge the world's technology leaders.

## Samsung

Samsung Electronics became not only a challenger but also a pioneer. Samsung Electronics Manufacturing was established in 1969. Technologically it lagged behind the Korean electronics companies that already existed. It established a technology partnership with the Japanese company Sanyo and a joint venture with the Japanese companies NEC and Sumitomo. In 1969 it sent 43 workers to Sanyo and 63 workers to NEC for training. At Sanyo they studied radio condenser speakers, deflecting coils, and transformers and at NEC they studied Braun tubes, vacuum tubes, and discharge tubes (Samsung, 2012).

In the early 1970s Samsung and its partners began mass-producing, selling domestically, and exporting electronic and electric goods. These included radios, black-and-white televisions, electric calculators, frost-free refrigerators, cassette players, and fans. Hobday (1995a) noted that Japanese firms provided know-how while Samsung provided low-cost labor, management, engineering, and overhead. By 1978 it had made 5 million televisions. Unfortunately, according to Chang (2008), Samsung's products at the time were often of low quality. For instance, its fans could break easily.

Samsung in the 1970s did not just copy Japanese technology but also performed its own R&D to learn production techniques. It lacked the technology to make color televisions. There was no domestic market for color televisions because Korean networks could not broadcast in color. In 1974 Samsung sought to buy Japanese color picture tubes but the Japanese producers said Samsung was too far behind to absorb the technical know-how (Chang, 2008). Samsung then took apart foreign color televisions to learn how to make them. Before the end of the 1970s it persuaded Matsushita to sell it color picture tubes and began manufacturing color televisions.

Sato (1997) observed that Samsung's grit in producing color televisions for export when there was no domestic market showed that it was committed to the government's plan that Korean conglomerates both export and follow Japan's industrial progression from radios to black-and-white televisions to color televisions. Chang noted that Sony was like a guinea pig providing guidance for companies like Samsung as to what products to move into next. Through trial and error, help from foreign buyers, and the purchase of the US company Ampherex, Samsung also learned to make microwave ovens. By the 1980s Samsung had become one of the leading microwave producers (Hobday, 1995a).

During the 1973 oil crisis, Samsung had difficulty obtaining semiconductors from Japan. This slowed the production of televisions and electronic goods. In 1974 Samsung founder Byung-Chull Lee acquired Korea Semiconductor and began producing chips. The quality was poor, though, and even Samsung divisions balked at using them. As Chang (2008) recounted, Lee brought in Japanese engineers to train his workers and sent his engineers to Japan every weekend to obtain training. In the 1980s Lee focused on memory chips because he believed that demand for these would rise as the information technology industry grew. Chang noted that he focused on DRAM semiconductors because economies of scale are strong in this area. To finance the heavy investment, Samsung's semiconductor division had a debt–equity ratio that reached 450% (Modi, 1989).

As Irwin (1996) observed, DRAMs are a standardized commodity whose market approaches the perfectly competitive ideal. Its product cycles are short and prices fall 80% within one or two years. In 1983 Samsung acquired technology from an American company, Micron, to make 64 K DRAMs. It studied this technology and also brought in Korean engineers trained in the United States to learn how to make the next-generation 256 K chips. In addition it established a research institute in the United States, where Korean engineers in the United States trained engineers from Samsung.

Chang (2008) recounted that the Samsung engineers followed their teachers around all day learning how to make semiconductors, and then in the evening reviewed their notes together. Upon returning to Korea, they worked day and night to manufacture 256 K chips. Their chips were superior to the 256 K chips made by the engineers in America (Chang, 2008). The diligence Samsung employees displayed supports Pecht and colleagues (1997) observation that Korean employees are dedicated to their companies' success.

In 1985 and 1986 chip prices collapsed. This was partly due to a downturn in demand and partly due to increased production by Japanese manufacturers. The downturn was so severe that most American producers exited the DRAM market. The Japanese producers were compelled by the Semiconductor Trade Agreement to restrict supply into the United States and to increase prices. As Irwin (1996) discussed, Korean producers were not restricted by the Semiconductor Trade Agreement and could sell as much as they wanted at the higher prices. They recycled their earnings into R&D and capital formation. In the early 1990s Samsung became the world's leading producer of DRAMs. It also began producing LCD panels and other components.

Despite these successes, Samsung consumer products in the early 1990s were considered low quality (Chang, 2008). Samsung was often an OEM for other brands. In 1993 Samsung's chairman, Kun-Hee Lee, son of founder Byung-Chull Lee, toured the world to assess Samsung's reputation. He was so dismayed that he called all Samsung managers to Frankfurt and told them to change everything except their wives and children. In 1995, when he learned that Samsung cellphones had quality problems, he assembled 150,000 of them in front of a factory and burned them all in front of 2,000 employees. Mr. Lee's words and actions were pivotal and led to quality improvements (Kelly, 2017). Samsung became a more popular consumer electronics brand than Sony.

## Anam/Amkor

Anam/Amkor (henceforth Anam) founder Hyang-Soo Kim, encouraged by the Korean government's endorsement of electronics, exported $200,000 in semiconductors in 1970.[16] His son Joo-Jin, a student at MIT, established contacts with American companies. In 1973 they arranged a licensing deal with Matsushita and became the first Korea company to produce color televisions. Anam began producing watches and audio equipment. It soon specialized in semiconductor packaging. These packages are the casing surrounding semiconductors and ICs. They include connections for circuit boards and provide protection against chemical contamination and other dangers.

For the first 10 years the company focused on assembly. It assimilated manual and semiautomated assembly techniques. Anam imported semiconductor wafers from America, packaged them, and sent them back to America. It started by importing transistors and in 1978 began importing ICs. American companies provided used machinery, engineering advice, and detailed instructions. Anam's advantage was in labor-intensive labor and it offered almost no advanced engineering or R&D (Hobday, 1995a).

Irwin (1996) reported a boom in semiconductor demand in 1982–1983. To meet this demand Anam worked on engineering with US firms and in 1984 started an engineering R&D section. This section directed process innovations such as task automation. American customers, eager to ensure quality, provided engineering advice. As Hobday (1995a) noted, the R&D division focused on working with customers, improving equipment, and installing and modifying precision machinery.

Hobday (1995a) reported that after 1985 Anam began offering specifications to customers. Foreign buyers provided general requirements and Anam designed and produced the product. Anam's engineers instituted process innovations and required foreign input only on complex packages. They purchased, installed, and adjusted the necessary equipment. Anam needed to improve quality in order to maintain exports.

After 1988 Anam reached the frontier of package manufacturing. It worked on product development with leading American companies. It also used computer modeling and statistical testing for quality control. It could implement product innovations to meet customer needs and employed 200 engineers (Hobday, 1995a).

---

[16] This section draws on Hobday (1995a).

## Other Companies

Other chaebols also specialized in electronics. The leader was Goldstar Company (now LG Electronics), founded in 1958. Goldstar obtained technical assistance from Japanese firms and produced transistor radios and radio tubes in the early 1960s. In 1962 Goldstar sent engineers to Hitachi for training and began exporting radios to the United States. In the 1970s Goldstar obtained technology through licensing and subcontracting arrangements with Japanese firms (Hobday, 1995a). It began mass-producing color televisions in 1977.

In the 1980s it focused on color televisions, microwave ovens, and video cassette recorders. It was the leading Korean electronics producer in 1981 and the second leading producer in 1987. It then advanced from consumer electronics to semiconductors. It licensed the technology from Hitachi (Hobday, 1995a). It has continued to grow and as of 2020 had more than 70,000 employees and assets of almost USD 40 billion.

Daewoo was a leading producer of color televisions, microwave ovens, and video cassette recorders in the 1980s. Hyundai Electronics (renamed SK Hynix) skipped consumer electronics and began directly producing computers and semiconductors in the mid-1980s (Modi, 1989). Daewoo and SK Hynix remain major electronics manufacturers as of 2020.

## Interpretation

As Taiwanese and Korean firms began producing electronic goods, Japanese firms transferred technology. Taiwanese firms in joint ventures or contract manufacturing relations with Japanese firms learned to make transistor radios and televisions. Japanese multinationals also sparked a network of parts suppliers in Taiwan. Unlike American MNCs, Japanese MNCs provided know-how and training to Korean firms as they started producing consumer electronics.

Sanyo and NEC, for instance, provided training in Japan to Samsung's workers. Japanese firms thus followed Kojima's (1973) model of transplanting superior production technology to developing countries through training workers and managers. Taiwanese and Korean engineers were adept at assimilating technologies, reverse engineering products, and innovating. Part of this was due to the governments' investment in education.

Taiwan and Korea both followed Japan's industrial progression from transistor radios, to black-and-white televisions, to color televisions, to more sophisticated consumer electronics and semiconductors (Modi, 1989; Sato, 1997). These two economies shared with Japan high national saving and investment rates, export-oriented economies, loyal and educated workers, and many other characteristics. The industries that Japanese firms had succeeded in when at comparable levels of development provided guidance to firms in Taiwan and Korea about promising opportunities. Entrepreneurs thus received the externality benefits that Hausmann and Rodrik (2003) highlighted as firms that pioneer new industries provide guidance to other firms about what an economy with a given endowment is good at producing.

Manufacturing semiconductors requires massive investment in physical capital and R&D. Since Taiwanese firms were not large enough to finance these investments, public–private partnerships were used. The semiconductor industry was promoted by ITRI in identifying and absorbing new technologies, training researchers, and spinning off companies. The Korean government promoted semiconductors and used a carrot-and-stick approach. It emphasized exports as necessary to survival and provided subsidized credit to exporting firms. If they succeeded at exporting, the credit continued. Samsung took the government's imperative seriously, learning to produce color televisions even when there was no protected domestic market to provide profits. In addition, as Pecht and colleagues (1997) observed, workers were patriotic and determined that Korea become an economic giant. The focus from top to bottom was thus that companies like Samsung succeed at exporting.

The promotion of the semiconductor industry by ITRI was successful. However, as Hobday, Cawson, and Kim (2001) noted, it is too simple to attribute this accomplishment to a large role for the government along a single state-market continuum. When the TAC hatched the plan for semiconductor development in 1974, Taiwan was in crisis. Not only was it still technically at war with the PRC, it had just left the United Nations, severed relations with a key source of technology and capital (Japan), and suffered a 47% increase in consumer prices from the first oil shock. Many overseas Chinese scholars, engineers, and researchers lined up to help Taiwan. As Lin and Rasiah (2014) observed, members of the TAC accepted no remuneration, got permission from their US companies to participate, used their vacation days to come and offer advice, and received only one round-trip ticket to Taiwan per year from the government.

The Taiwanese government at this time focused on development in order to survive. Willett (1995) highlighted that, when national security concerns become paramount, the polity reacts as a unified actor. Agents in the political arena take action for the good of the nation. At other times, interest group competition, rent-seeking, and distributional struggles can predominate.

Wagner (1993) emphasized that it is not only the incentives of government officials that matter when they intervene in the marketplace but also their knowledge. Taiwan in the early 1970s accessed knowledge both from the overseas Taiwanese diaspora and from scholars born in mainland China who had left to escape the revolution. For instance, Wen-yuan Pan, Ta-Chung Liu, and Sho-Chieh Tsiang were all world-class scholars born in mainland China. Taiwan's population at the time was less than 16 million and its diaspora was small. China's population was almost 900 million and its diaspora was enormous. Taiwan had access to an exceptional knowledge base that provided advice free of charge.

South Korea in the 1970s and 1980s faced 750,000 troops on its northern border, infiltration incidents, and attempted assassinations. The threat of imminent invasion was always credible. Economic development promoted national security in the face of this threat (Dee, 1984). This helps explain the patriotism just mentioned. For Korea as well as Taiwan, the unified actor framework provides a better way to model political economy interactions in this crisis period than a framework highlighting rent-seeking and interest group competition.

The importance of entrepreneurs is seen in Samsung chairman Byung-Chul Lee's prioritizing and investing in DRAM production and his son Kun-Hee Lee's insistence that Samsung improve quality. Kun-Hee's "Frankfurt Declaration" was so influential that it was recorded in a book given to Samsung employees and set the stage for Samsung becoming a world leader (Kelly, 2017).

The importance of worker migration in transplanting know-how is seen by the return of many successful researchers from the United States to work in Taiwan. They brought the skills they acquired back with them and retained contacts in the United States who helped them with technical problems. The close proximity of electronics firms, HSBIP, ITRI, National Tsing Hua University, and National Chiao Tung University meant that scientists, researchers, and engineers could be in close contact with their peers. They would also migrate from firm to firm, as when employees left Microtek and produced scanners elsewhere, allowing their human capital to spread. As Yoshitomi (2003) observed, this leads to a virtuous cycle of growth. Taiwanese firms transitioned from manufacturing televisions to making computer monitors. This illustrates Hausmann and colleagues' (2013) insight that, as monkeys jump to close trees, economies migrate to producing goods that require similar know-how.

## 4 The Little Tigers Emerge

Between 1985 and 1988 the Japanese yen appreciated by 60% in real terms against the US dollar. Between 1986 and 1989, the Korean won and New Taiwan dollar both appreciated by 37% against the US dollar. Rural–urban migration also evaporated in Korea and Taiwan at this time, causing wages to

soar (Yoshitomi, 2003). In addition the United States withdrew tariff conces-
sions to Korea and Taiwan offered under the Generalized System of Preferences
(GSP) in 1989. Japan, Korea, and Taiwan thus faced serious challenges to their
price competitiveness in the late 1980s.

They responded by transferring factories to lower-cost locations in Malaysia,
the Philippines, Thailand, and other places. They continued to produce sophisticated P&C domestically, and exported these to ASEAN for assembly and
reexport. This is clear in Figures 7 and 8, which show a surge of electronic P&C
exports from Japan, South Korea, and Taiwan to ASEAN countries after 1985.
Incipient value chains then emerged in the region.

One way to understand these value chains is to study a specific example. The
next section examines the emergence of the hard disk drive (HDD) value chain.

### The Hard Disk Drive Value Chain in Thailand

In 1982 an HDD manufacturer, Seagate, commenced production in Singapore.
As Hiratsuka (2011) noted, Seagate was attracted by a 5-year tax exemption, the
presence of many foreign suppliers, the abundance of English-speaking engineers, and a cluster of HDD users such as Digital Equipment Corporation and
Apple. Singapore, like Taiwan and Korea, experienced a large appreciation and
rising wages beginning in the late 1980s. Seagate moved HDD assembly in
1987 to Chok Chai, Thailand. Seagate was attracted by an 11-year tax holiday
and low labor costs (Hiratsuka, 2011; Hobday and Rush, 2007). IBM began

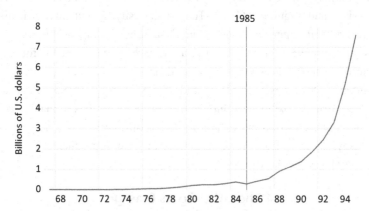

**Figure 7** Japanese electronic P&C exports to Malaysia, the Philippines, and
Thailand

**Note:** Electronic P&C are from International Standard Industrial Code (ISIC) classification
3210.

**Source:** CEPII-CHELEM database

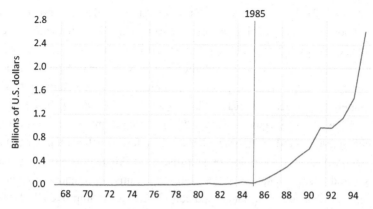

**Figure 8** Korea and Taiwan's electronic P&C exports to Malaysia, the
Philippines, and Thailand
**Note:** Electronic P&C are from International Standard Industrial Code (ISIC) classification
3210.
**Source:** CEPII-CHELEM database

HDD assembly in Thailand in 1991. Fujitsu and Western Digital also migrated
to Thailand, creating a large cluster of HDD assemblers. IBM's operations were
later acquired by Hitachi.

Hiratsuka (2011) documented where Hitachi acquired the P&C to produce
HDDs. He reported that it purchased the same P&C from many firms in different
countries. For instance, it sourced media from Hoya in Japan, Komag in
Malaysia, Hoya in Singapore, and Hitachi in China and the United States. It
sourced PCBs from Solectron in Indonesia, Bridgestone in Japan, Ionix in the
Philippines, Global Brands Manufacture and Sanmina in China, and Sanmina in
Thailand. It sourced pivots from firms in Malaysia, Singapore, and Thailand;
voice coils from firms in Indonesia, Malaysia, and Thailand; and bases from firms
in Malaysia, China, and Thailand. In Thailand it relied more on Japanese firms
than on indigenous firms, and much of the sourcing was from other firms rather
than from Hitachi affiliates. Hiratsuka found that only for core components such
as silicon wafers and thin chip sliders did Hitachi rely on imports from Hitachi
affiliates abroad.

Hiratsuka (2011) reported that Hitachi employed a just-in-time (JIT)
system when procuring P&C. Suppliers paid for goods from Thailand and
overseas to arrive in a JIT warehouse close to the Hitachi plant. The P&C
were delivered four times per day to the plant and the goods were counted as
delivered when they left the warehouse. Hitachi, its suppliers, and the
warehouse were all connected online so all could see when particular parts
were running low.

Hiratsuka (2011) reported that Hitachi sourced primarily from firms within a three-hour drive or located in nearby countries. This facilitated communication between supplier firms and Hitachi and the resolution of problems related to defective parts. A Japanese parts supplier in Malaysia, for instance, routinely sent engineers to the Hitachi plant to communicate with counterparts and immediately dispatched technical workers when defective parts were delivered.

Kohpaiboon and Poapongsakorn (2011) reported intensive cooperation between suppliers and HDD manufacturers. A few supplier employees met daily with HDD maker employees and discussed production efficiency, cost savings, and possible changes. These interfirm teams coordinated production schedules, evaluated performance, and considered how to improve HDD quality. The HDD makers sometimes requested that suppliers change their tier-2 suppliers when parts were defective. Makers evaluated suppliers and determined future orders by their speed in responding to these requests. Since HDD manufacturers could see the entire production process, they were well placed to make requests from specific suppliers.

Kohpaiboon and Poapongsakorn (2011) also noted that suppliers had to have an individual production line for each HDD manufacturer. Because product life cycles are short and demand is unpredictable, HDD manufacturers had to be prepared for uncharted opportunities. Tier-1 suppliers therefore had to retain excess capacity and be ready to implement new R&D innovations. There was a close and symbiotic relationship between HDD makers and their suppliers.

Kohpaiboon and Poapongsakorn (2011) noted upgrading in Thailand's HDD sector. Initially, Thai workers were only able to assemble P&C. Thai workers at MNC affiliates later developed the ability to construct prototypes, adapt designs for production, order tools, and assign tasks. They could conduct pilot runs and observe problems before engaging in mass production. Carrying out these activities required many engineers and scientists.

Hobday and Rush (2007) outlined how this upgrading occurred at Seagate's Thailand affiliate. In 1982 Seagate in Thailand established a plant of 50 employees, benefiting from low labor costs. Its operations expanded with the establishment of the Chok Chai plant in 1987. As the work was technical, foreign engineers trained Thai engineers. Hobday and Rush reported that as Thai engineers gained experience, they in turn trained Thai engineers and technicians and workers learned the art of HDD manufacturing.

In 1989 engineers oversaw the start-up and installation of capital goods at a new plant in Teparuk. They also handled quality control and software development (Hobday and Rush, 2007). Competition with other HDD manufacturers forced Seagate engineers to implement process innovations. As an example, teams were formed to analyze defects in production. Each team felt responsible for an individual production process. When yields fell below 98%, they stopped the production line to analyze the problem. Within four weeks they could raise yields to 99.5–99.6% (Hobday and Rush, 2007).

By the late 1990s employees at Teparuk received four weeks of training per year. When new product lines were introduced operators received classroom training followed by on-the-job training. Engineers and technicians also received instruction, and the training was done in the Thai language. Seagate also supported R&D at the Asian Institute of Technology in Bangkok and received trained technicians from this university (Hobday and Rush, 2007).

One weakness is that this upgrading has occurred at affiliates of MNCs. Local Thai companies have had difficulty joining the HDD supply chain (Kohpaiboon and Poapongsakorn, 2011). Malaysia has also experienced difficulty linking indigenous firms to global value chains, especially outside of the state of Penang.

## The Electronics Industry in Malaysia

In the late 1960s and early 1970s the Malaysian government took several steps to attract labor-intensive assembly activities (Rasiah, 1999a, 1999b).[17] It opened free trade zones, starting with Bayan Lepas, Penang, in 1972. These provided tariff exemptions, 5–10-year tax holidays, and investment tax credits. The government also provided subsidized land, water, electricity, and infrastructure, restricted union activities, and promised to safeguard the interest of MNCs. In addition the Penang Development Corporation (PDC) in the 1970s wooed manufacturing firms such as Intel and Motorola to Penang. As Rasiah noted, these policies plus good infrastructure, responsiveness to MNCs, political stability, and an English-speaking workforce led to a wave of inward FDI in the 1970s. Advanced Micro Devices, Agilent Technologies, Clarion, Fairchild Semiconductor, Hitachi Semiconductors, Intel, Osram Opto Services, and Robert Services all set up operations in Bayan Lepas (Chai and Im, 2009). Other MNCs establishing operations in Malaysia included Hewlett-Packard, Motorola, and Siemens. As Freund and Moran (2017) noted, firms in Malaysia at this time specialized in assembling simple devices (e.g., PCBs) and manufacturing consumer goods (e.g., black-and-white televisions).

The second wave of FDI started with the appreciations of the Japanese yen, Korean won, Singapore dollar, and New Taiwan dollar and the revocation of GSP privileges from the newly industrialized economies. The Malaysian government also offered incentives to attract FDI under the Investment Promotion Act of 1986 such as allowing 100% equity ownership for foreign firms that export at least 50% of their output, employ 350 Malaysian workers, and do not

---

[17] This section draws on the writings of Professor Rajah Rasiah.

compete with Malaysian firms (Chai and Im, 2009). These pull and push factors succeeded, and Malaysia's FDI inflows grew at an annual average rate of 38.7% between 1986 and 1996 (Karimi and Yusop, 2009).

These inflows led to the development of indigenous supplier firms and learning, especially in Penang. The PDC and MNCs located in Bayan Lepas established the Penang Skills Development Corporation in 1989 to train workers. These MNCs also sourced parts and offered guidance to local firms in Penang. Rasiah (2017) noted that intense competition forced firms to introduce automation, statistical quality control, and JIT inventory practices. The JIT practices required supplier firms to locate close to the producers. A vibrant industrial cluster emerged and suppliers such as Globetronics Techology, Eng Technology, Atlan Industries, and LKT Automation became international firms (Chai and Im, 2009).

Outside of Penang local firms were less successful at linking with MNCs and obtaining technology transfers. Instead, the MNCs sourced largely from non-Malaysian companies. Indigenous companies also performed little R&D (Rasiah, 1999a, 2003).

In the IC industry, the largest sector within the Malaysian electronics industry, local firms were mired in lower-value-added activities such as assembly and testing. The Malaysian government sought to imitate Korea and Taiwan by using industrial policy to raise Malaysian firms into higher-value-added activities such as R&D, design, and fabrication (Rasiah, 2017). It established the Malaysian Institute of Microelectronics Systems (MIMOS) in 1985 to promote national semiconductor firms, and MIMOS conceived of a Malaysian semiconductor fabrication firm and acquired very large-scale integration technology to facilitate this. It then created Silterra in 2000 in the Kulim High Tech Park.

However, Silterra did not emerge as a cutting-edge producer of semiconductors as TSMC did in Taiwan and Samsung did in Korea. Rasiah (2010, 2017) has discussed why this is so. Malaysian politics is dominated by preferences to promote indigenous Malaysians (*bumiputera*) over ethnic Chinese and Indian Malaysians. Thus, when choosing key personnel to lead Silterra, high-tech parks, and other institutions, Malaysia did not follow the Taiwanese model of choosing the best candidates. For instance, while Taiwan tapped Morris Chang, who had been vice president at Texas Instruments, to lead TSMC, Malaysia did not choose Loh Kin Wah, the experienced managing director of Qimonda, for a leadership role (Rasiah, 2017). The Malaysian government also showed reluctance in providing grants to ethnic Chinese firms, even though these were dynamic in the electronics sector. In addition, it did not follow Korea's example of withholding benefits to firms who failed to export or meet other performance targets. Finally, the educational system failed to create enough high-quality engineers and scientists. Admission to universities was influenced strongly by the politics of ethnicity.

Further, universities, research institutes, and semiconductor firms did not establish close links as they had in Taiwan. For instance, Heng Huck Lee, the head of Globetronics, said that university research remained confined to the university and that companies were unable to tap into the brains of academics (*The Star*, 2014). Thus the industrial policy experience in Malaysia was not as successful as in Taiwan and Korea and Malaysia remains mired in middle-income status.

## The Asian Financial Crisis

By the 1990s the success of Japan, South Korea, Taiwan, and ASEAN at export-led industrialization had become legendary. For instance, in 1993 the World Bank published a book entitled *The East Asian Miracle*. The region's success spawned irrational exuberance and investors flooded the area with portfolio capital.

As Yoshitomi (2003) observed, much of this capital was short-term and denominated in US dollars. As funds poured in, banks and firms in East Asia lacked sufficient risk-management skills and supervisors lacked prudential financial regulatory capacity. Short-term dollar-denominated liabilities such as Japanese bank loans flowed to long-term local currency–denominated assets such as apartment buildings in Bangkok. The Thai baht, Indonesian rupiah, and Malaysian ringgit were pegged to the US dollar. The ASEAN firms discounted the risk of currency depreciations, as evidenced by the fact that their foreign currency borrowing remained unhedged.

The capital inflows produced asset market bubbles. Yoshitomi (2003) documented that stock prices in Indonesia, Malaysia, and Thailand more than doubled between 1991 and 1993 and that property prices almost doubled in Indonesia, tripled in Malaysia, and increased four and a half times in Thailand over this period.

A series of negative shocks then hit ASEAN economies. The Chinese renminbi depreciated by 40% against the US dollar in 1994, increasing the competition ASEAN firms faced from firms exporting from China. The Japanese yen depreciated by 33% against the US dollar beginning in April 1995. Since ASEAN currencies were pegged to the dollar, they appreciated relative to the Japanese yen. This caused ASEAN exporters to lose price competitiveness in Japan, one of their crucial markets. The electronics industry also experienced a downturn due to oversupply.

Speculators attacked Thailand, Malaysia, and Indonesia's dollar pegs in 1997. There were massive reversals of capital flows, equaling 16.7% of GDP for Thailand and 13.4% of GDP for Indonesia (Yoshitomi and Ohno, 1999). The asset bubbles burst, with the Thai property index falling from 367 in 1993 to 7 in 1997 and the Indonesian property index falling from 214 in 1993 to 40 in 1997 (Yoshitomi, 2003). Central banks abandoned their dollar pegs. The Thai baht and Malaysian ringgit depreciated by 30% against the US dollar and the Indonesian rupiah fell from 2,400 to the dollar before the attack to 14,900 against the dollar in June 1998.

The balance sheets of firms and banks with foreign currency liabilities deteriorated and they lost access to credit. Without working capital, they had to restrict economic activity. The ASEAN economies experienced severe recessions. There were riots in Indonesia and President Suharto was forced to resign. This crisis atmosphere detracted from the locational advantages of investing in ASEAN. The ASEAN travails plus China's accession to the WTO in 2001 redirected FDI from Southeast Asia to China.

## Interpretation

The ASEAN experience indicates how FDI is influenced both by push and by pull factors. The appreciations in Japan, Korea, Singapore, and Taiwan and the expiration of GSP preferences and rising wages in the newly industrialized economies (NIEs) caused firms in these countries to look outward for factory locations. Malaysia and Thailand attracted FDI with their low-wage workers, placid labor unions, acceptable infrastructure, tax holidays, free trade zones that were exempt from tariffs and offered subsidized infrastructure, English-speaking workers, and other locational advantages.

Hitachi's procurement of P&C illustrates the slicing up of the value chain. It sourced many parts from firms located nearby. There was close coordination between Hitachi and its Tier-1 suppliers, with daily meetings focused on improving efficiency. In addition, JIT inventory management with all parties monitoring stocks continuously allowed firms to minimize costs. Having several suppliers for each part also gave Hitachi bargaining power that it used to improve quality and reduce costs. However, having several suppliers in diverse countries is against the prediction of production network theory that emphasizes that each component should be produced in the location with a comparative advantage in producing that component (Hiratsuka, 2011).

The previous section indicated that Taiwan and South Korea were successful at using industrial policy to advance their semiconductor industries to the frontier. This section records how Malaysia failed although it took many of the same steps. A crucial difference is in the nature of the political equilibrium.

Taiwan and Korea in the 1970s faced threats of invasion and deep economic crises. Political leaders, citizens, and overseas Chinese and Koreans were all determined to see their economies succeed as a way to promote national security. In this situation, actors in the political arena united to promote the national welfare.

Malaysia, on the other hand, had overcome threats of rural unrest after two decades of strong growth. The government was focused on redistributing wealth and firm ownership to the *bumiputera*. When making decisions on leadership at semiconductor companies, admissions to college, and grants to firms, it did not choose the most qualified candidates. The emphasis on redistribution also led to rent-seeking activities. In this environment industrial policy failed to accomplish structural transformation.

## 5 The Dragon Stirs

In December 1978 Chairman Deng Xiaoping announced that China would open up to foreign investment. As Tuan and Ng (2004) documented, China revolutionized its value system and its institutional and socioeconomic structure in order to attract FDI. It instituted business-friendly laws in areas such as joint ventures, wholly owned subsidiaries, income taxes, and insurance. It established special economic zones (SEZs) that offered lower taxes, reduced regulations, and other benefits to foreign firms. Two of the key SEZs were the Pearl and Yangtze River deltas. China built superb highways, ports, airports, and other infrastructure in these areas. It also earned the confidence of foreign investors by maintaining consistent policies (Tuan and Ng, 2004).

China joined the WTO in 2001. Joining the WTO increased the confidence of foreign investors that China would maintain consistent policies and respect the rule of law. China also liberalized FDI regulations as part of its WTO protocols. These changes offered preferential tax rates, duty-free import of equipment and goods, and other benefits in "encouraged" sectors (Inada and Guo, 2016). Many electronic goods were in encouraged sectors.

A sea change in China's electronics imports and exports followed. To explain this the next section discusses the specific case of the offshoring of Taiwan's notebook PC industry to the Yangtze River delta.

### The Notebook Cluster in the Yangtze River Delta

Taiwan liberalized outgoing FDI to China in 2001. Before this, it followed a "patience over haste" policy that limited investments in high-technology sectors to a percentage of a firm's capital with a ceiling of USD 50 million. In 2001 this was replaced by an "active opening and effective management" policy that removed the dollar limit and regularly raised restrictions on investments (Tsou, Liu, Hammitt, and Chang, 2013).

Yoshitomi (2006) discussed the offshoring of notebook manufacturing from Taiwan to the Yangtze River delta. Under the active opening policy, Taiwan deregulated outward FDI into China from notebook manufacturers. Original design manufacturers (ODMs) were attracted by low wages and good infrastructure in the Yangtze River delta.

Between 50 and 100 Taiwanese suppliers migrated to China. These firms provided connectors, batteries, switches, and displays and had up to 10,000 employees per firm. Employees from ODMs trained workers at supplier firms. The ODMs produced for brands such as Hewlett-Packard, Apple, and Toshiba. Microprocessors were provided by companies such as Intel and operating systems were provided by companies such as Microsoft. Yoshitomi (2006) noted that several thousand SMEs in the cluster engaged in casting, forging, plating, module assembling, and similar activities. On average these firms employed a few hundred employees.

The ODMs faced risks. Technology improved at lightning speed. Tastes and preferences changed. Product cycles were short. To handle these uncertainties firms adopted real-time management systems that covered every aspect of production. Customized made-to-order requests were processed using computer technology. Some ODMs kept inventories lean by processing 98% of orders within three days. This value chain experienced mushrooming productivity growth.

Dedrick, Kraemer, and Linden (2010) noted that many assemblers and suppliers within the notebook PC value chain did not have market power. Assemblers could switch suppliers and the abundance of suppliers implied that assemblers competed fiercely with each other. On the other hand, they observed that Intel and Microsoft possessed market power when providing processors and software for PCs.

Hewlett-Packard outsourced much of its manufacturing to Taiwanese ODMs in China. Dedrick, Kraemer, and Linden (2010) reported the results from a teardown of the inputs into the Hewlett-Packard nc6230 Notebook PC in 2005. They reported a factory cost of USD 856.33. For US companies, Intel earned $205.43 (24.0%) for the main chipset and Wi-Fi, Microsoft earned $100.00 (11.7%) for the Windows XP Pro OEM license, ATI Technologies earned $20.50 (2.4%) for the graphics processor, Texas Instruments earned $3.28 (0.4%) for the cardbus controller, Broadcom earned $2.01 (0.2%) for the Ethernet controller with the transceiver, Standard Microsystems earned $1.42 (0.2%) for the I/O controller, and Texas Instruments earned $1.22 (0.1%) for the battery charge controller.

For Japanese companies, Toshiba Matsushita Display earned $137.14 (16.0%) for the Display Assembly, Fujitsu earned $68.00 (7.9%) for the 60GB hard drive, an unspecified company earned $40.52 (4.7%) for the battery pack, and Matsushita earned $40.00 (4.7%) for the DVD-ROM/CD-RW Drive. Among Korean firms, Samsung earned $29.65 (3.5%) for the memory board and Hynix Semiconductor earned $5.68 (0.7%) for the DDR SDRAM Memory. Other parts then contributed $177.72 (20.8%) and assembly and testing contributed $23.76 (2.8%). Dedrick, Kraemer, and Linden (2010) estimated the wholesale price (after discounts) received by Hewlett-Packard at $1,189, yielding Hewlett Packard a gross margin of 28% ($333/$1,189). They reported similar results for the Lenovo ThinkPad T43 Notebook PC in 2005.

These findings indicate that, despite soaring productivity within this value chain, little of the income accrued to Chinese workers. Dosi, Virgillito, and Yu (2020) reported that the elasticity of real wages with respect to labor productivity was small at this time. They attributed this to the massive flow of migrant workers from inland provinces to work in manufacturing jobs in the coastal regions.

## Apple

In the 1990s Apple Computer lost out as consumers favored personal computers running Microsoft software and using Intel microprocessors. Apple brought Steve Jobs back in 1997 and made him CEO in 2000. Apple began work on a music player at this time and Jobs devoted 100% of his time to this project (Kahney, 2004). In October 2001 Jobs introduced the iPod as a digital music player that enabled listeners to carry their entire music collection in their pockets and listen to it wherever they went. Apple decided to use available components to construct the iPod rather than custom-designed parts (Sherman, 2002). Apple also assembled the iPod in China using Taiwanese contract manufacturers.

Dedrick, Kraemer, and Linden (2010) reported the results from a teardown of the inputs into the 30GB 5th-Generation iPod in 2005. They found a factory cost of USD 144.56. For Japanese companies, Toshiba earned $73.39 (51%) for the hard drive, Toshiba–Matsushita Display earned $23.27 (16%) for the display assembly, an unspecified Japanese company earned $2.89 for the battery pack, and Elpida earned $1.85 (1%) for the mobile RAM. For US companies, Broadcom earned $8.36 (6%) for the multimedia player, PortalPlayer earned $4.94 (3%) for the controller chip, and Spansion earned $0.84 (1%) for the flash memory.

For Korean companies, Samsung earned $2.37 (2%) for the SDRAM memory. Other parts then contributed $22.79 (16%) and assembly and testing contributed $3.86 (3%). Dedrick, Kraemer, and Linden (2010) estimated the wholesale price (after discounts) received by Apple at $224, yielding Apple a gross margin of 29% ($80/$224). For iPods sold through Apple's website or stores, Apple received an additional $45, yielding a gross margin of 56%.

Dedrick, Kraemer, and Linden's (2010) findings again imply that little of the income generated from the iPod accrued to Chinese workers. They noted that it took 10 minutes to assemble an iPod and that Chinese workers could earn as little as $0.01 a minute.

Apple introduced the iPhone in 2007 and the iPad in 2010. It assembled these products through the Taiwanese company Foxconn in China. Kraemer, Linden, and Dedrick (2011) reported a teardown analysis for these products. For the iPhone 4 in 2010, the retail price was USD 549. Of this, $321 accrued to Apple. Suppliers in the United States then earned $13, suppliers in Japan $3, suppliers in Korea $26, suppliers in Taiwan $3, and suppliers in the European Union $6. Chinese workers earned $10 for assembly of the iPhone and the components going into it. For the 16 GB WiFi iPad in 2010, the retail price was USD 424. Of this, $150 accrued to Apple. Suppliers in the United States then earned $12, suppliers in Japan $7, suppliers in Korea $34, suppliers in Taiwan $7, and suppliers in the EU $1. Chinese workers earned $10 for assembly of the iPad and for the components going into it.

## The Evolution of Regional Value Chains

The combination of entrepreneurs such as Steve Jobs, competitively priced P&C produced in upstream Asian economies and elsewhere, and low wages and good infrastructure in China proved unbeatable. Figure 9 shows the value of exports of FEGs (i.e., computers, phones, and consumer electronic goods) from the leading exporters. China's exports took off after China joined the WTO in 2001. By 2007 the value of China's FEG exports equaled $318 billion, more than the value of FEG exports from the next 5 countries. After 2007 China's FEG exports soared and eventually surpassed FEG exports from the next 14 leading exporters.

Figure 10 shows electronic parts and components (EP&C) exports from East Asia to individual East Asian countries and regions. Before 2001 these flowed largely to ASEAN, Korea, and Taiwan. After China's WTO accession, however, they flowed disproportionately to China. Japan, being upstream in regional value chains, received small quantities of P&C from other Asian countries.

Figure 11 shows EP&C exports from Taiwan to East Asia. It highlights the slicing up of the value chain that occurred after Taiwan deregulated outward FDI to China and after China joined the WTO and deregulated inward FDI. Taiwanese firms continued producing sophisticated P&C domestically and shipping these to China for assembly.

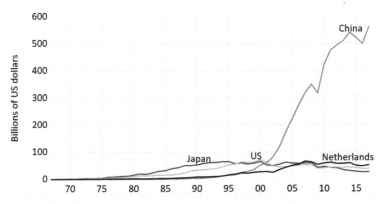

**Figure 9** Final electronic goods exports from leading exporters
**Note:** Final electronic goods include consumer electronics, computer equipment, and telecommunications equipment.
**Source:** CEPII-CHELEM database

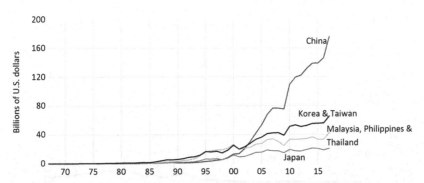

**Figure 10** Electronic P&C exports from East Asia to East Asian regions and countries
**Note:** Electronic P&Cs come from International Standard Industrial Classification Code 3210. East Asia includes China, Japan, South Korea, Taiwan, and the ASEAN countries.
**Source:** CEPII-CHELEM database.

Figure 12 shows Korea's exports, Figure 13 shows Japan's, and Figure 14 shows ASEAN's. For Korea, the figure indicates how important providing components to firms operating in China became after China's WTO accession. For Japan, the figure also indicates an increase in P&C exports to China around the turn of the millennium. Japan's EP&C exports were much more diversified across East Asia than those from Korea and Taiwan. Japan and China's relations are fraught with conflict and this causes Japan to diversify its assembly operations. For Malaysia, the Philippines, and Thailand P&C exports became more

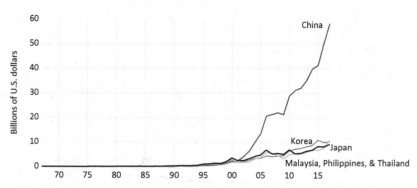

**Figure 11** Electronic P&C exports from Taiwan to East Asian regions and
countries

**Note:** Electronic P&Cs come from International Standard Industrial Classification Code
3210.

**Source:** CEPII-CHELEM database

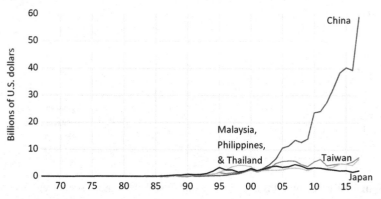

**Figure 12** Electronic P&C exports from South Korea to East Asian regions and
countries

**Note:** Electronic P&C comes from International Standard Industrial Classification Code
3210.

**Source:** CEPII-CHELEM database

focused on China after 2000. Much of this was from MNCs operating in
ASEAN (e.g., Hitachi producing hard disk drives in Thailand).

## *Exchange Rates and China's Exports*

China's exports to the United States increased from $82 billion in 1999 to
$338 billion in 2008. Its trade surplus with the United States increased from

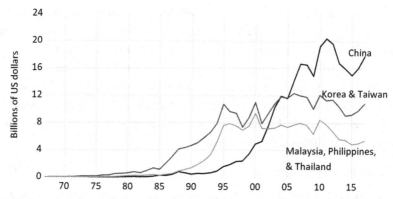

**Figure 13** Electronic P&C exports from Japan to East Asian regions and countries

**Note:** Electronic P&Cs come from International Standard Industrial Classification Code 3210.

**Source:** CEPII-CHELEM database

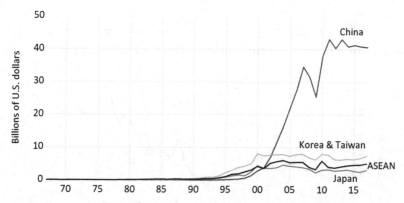

**Figure 14** Electronic P&C exports from Malaysia, the Philippines, and Thailand to East Asian regions and countries

**Note:** Electronic P&Cs come from International Standard Industrial Classification Code 3210

**Source:** CEPII-CHELEM database

$69 billion in 1999 to $268 billion in 2008. China kept its exchange rates fixed to the US dollar until July 2005, allowed it to appreciate until August 2008, and then kept it fixed to the dollar during the GFC. Many argued that the renminbi was undervalued and this drove China's export juggernaut.

However, the Chinese yuan has appreciated significantly after 2005 as China's exports have soared. On the other hand, exchange rates in upstream countries producing much of the value-added have depreciated. To calculate exchange rates in supply chain countries, we can focus on the nine leading suppliers of EP&C to China. These are Japan, South Korea, Taiwan, Malaysia, Singapore, Thailand, the Philippines, Germany, and the United States. For these suppliers, weights are calculated by dividing the value of their EP&C exports to China by the value of EP&C exports coming from all nine suppliers together. These weights are used to calculate an exchange rate index in supply chain countries (SSRER) using the equation:

$$SSRER_t = SSRER_{t-1} \amalg_i (REER_{i,t}/ REER_{i,t-1})^{w_{i,t}} \qquad (2),$$

where $REER_{i,t}$ is the real effective exchange rate in supply chain country $i$ at time $t$ and $w_{i,t}$ is the share of EP&C exports coming from supply chain country $i$ relative to all nine supply chain countries.

Figure 15 plots both the renminbi real effective exchange rate and the exchange rate index for supply chain countries. The figure indicates that, while the renminbi appreciated 43% between the second quarter of 2005 and the second quarter of 2022, the index of exchange rates in supply chain countries depreciated by 6% over this period.

Ahmed (2009) investigated how the renminbi exchange rate and exchange rates in supply chain countries affect China's processed exports that are

**Figure 15** The renminbi real effective exchange rate and an exchange rate index for countries supplying EP&C to China

**Notes:** The exchange rate index for supply chain countries is a geometrically weighted average of real effective exchange rates in the nine leading suppliers of EP&C. The nine leading suppliers are Japan, South Korea, Taiwan, Malaysia, Singapore, Thailand, the Philippines, Germany, and the United States. The weights are determined by the share of P&C flowing from each of these economies to China each year.
**Source:** Bank for International Settlements, CEPII-CHELEM database, CEIC database, and calculations by the author

produced using imported P&C. He employed an auto-regressive distributed lag framework and quarterly data over the 1996–2009 period. He reported that a 10% appreciation of the renminbi would reduce processed exports by 15% and a 10% appreciation on East Asian supply chain countries would reduce processed exports by 17%. He concluded that a unilateral appreciation of the renminbi would affect China's exports much less than an appreciation of exchange rates throughout the supply chain.

Thorbecke and Smith (2010) employed panel dynamic ordinary least squares (DOLS) techniques and data on China's exports to 33 countries over the 1994 to 2004 period. They reported that a 10% renminbi appreciation would reduce processed exports by less than 4% and that a 10% appreciation throughout the supply chain would reduce processed exports by 10%.

Yamashita and Jayasuriya (2013) investigated China's exports to OECD countries disaggregated at the Standard Industrial Trade Classification (SITC) two-digit industry level over the 1992–2009 period. They used the weighted exchange rate between China and nine East Asian economies (Japan, Hong Kong, Taiwan, South Korea, Singapore, Malaysia, Indonesia, Thailand, and the Philippines). They obtained weights based on the share of P&C coming into China from each of these economies.

Yamashita and Jayasuriya (2013) also employed the bilateral real exchange rate between China and each OECD importing country. They found that for exports of electronics and transport equipment (SITC category 7 goods), a 10% renminbi appreciation relative to East Asian supply chain countries would decrease exports by 11.5% and a 10% appreciation relative to an importing country would reduce exports by 12.4%. If the renminbi and exchange rates in supply chain countries appreciated together against the OECD importing country's currency, their results imply that there would be a much larger drop in China's SITC category 7 exports than if the renminbi appreciated alone.

Thorbecke (2017) reported that 80% of China's merchandise trade surplus came from trade in FEGs consisting of computers, telecommunications equipment, and consumer electronics. Much of the value-added of China's FEG exports comes from microchips, sensors, and other P&C coming from East Asia. Using China's FEG exports to 20 countries and panel DOLS estimation over the 2002–2014 period, he found that a 10% appreciation in supply chain countries would reduce FEG exports by 14.5% and that a 10% appreciation of the renminbi would reduce FEG exports by 7.6%.

Thus after China's WTO accession in 2001, much of the value-added of China's sophisticated exports came from imported P&C. This implies that exchange rates in supply chain countries matter along with the renminbi for

China's exports. Since exchange rates in supply chain countries have depreciated since 2005 while the renminbi has appreciated significantly, upstream
exchange rates rather than the renminbi have contributed to the surge of
China's exports in recent years.

## Interpretation

China took several steps to attract FDI. It imposed business-friendly laws,
established SEZs with low taxes and reduced regulation, constructed superb
infrastructure, and joined the WTO. Joining the WTO reassured investors
that China would follow the rule of law. Taking these steps reduced the
service link cost of establishing production blocks in China, and MNCs
moved factories to China. Before the GFC China also had the locational
advantage of low-wage labor. Multinationals continued to produce P&C in
upstream Asian countries, but assembled the final goods in China. By 2008
China's final electronics exports exceeded those of the next 14 leading
exporters combined. In spite of the huge volume of exports, however,
China's value-added was low.

China's low value-added mitigated the impact of a renminbi appreciation on
China's exports. A concerted appreciation across East Asian supplier countries
would impact the price competitiveness of China's exports much more.

Value chains centered in China exhibit intricate cooperation among hundreds
of firms in several countries. At the same time, competition among suppliers and
final producers generates efficient management systems, lean inventories, and
mushrooming productivity.

# 6 Free-for-All

After the GFC firms gained access to ready-to-go modules to assemble TVs,
cellphones, and other electronic goods. In this digital world technological
prowess mattered less than ruthless cost cutting. Competition intensified and
generated destructive price wars. The United States, inundated with Asian
exports, began a trade war with China in 2018. Into this maelstrom the
COVID-19 pandemic arrived in 2020.

## Flat-Panel Displays and Televisions

Under the Digital Transition and Public Safety Act of 2005, the United States
required that television broadcasting switch from analog to digital by 2009.
Other countries mandated similar changes. Televisions using CRTs thus had to
be replaced by televisions using technologies such as LCD or plasma screens.

The LCD televisions soon outsold the plasma televisions by seven to one (Harding and Kwong, 2009). Sony, long dominant in CRT technologies such as Trinitron, was slow to switch to LCDs and depended on other companies to supply these panels (Harding, 2008). Sharp, a pioneer in LCD panel manufacturing, built the world's largest LCD plant in 2007. It invested $4.4 billion, more than one-third of its shareholders' equity, in the factory (Kwong, 2012). The plant could produce six 60-inch or fifteen 40-inch panels from one sheet of glass (Sanchanta, 2007).

Sharp pioneered LCD manufacturing and its ability to produce panels allowed it to vertically integrate television manufacturing. Large-screen (e.g., 40-inch and 60-inch) TVs were the most expensive. Sharp, along with Sony, Panasonic, and other Japanese firms, focused on selling these high-value-added and high-priced TVs to advanced countries (Sato et al., 2013). In the past Japanese firms used advanced technology to produce high-end products to avoid strenuous price competition.

In the first decade of the twenty-first century, however, Japanese electronics firms encountered fierce competition from Korean and Taiwanese firms. Samsung and LG in Korea and AU Optronics and Chi Mei Optoelectronics in Taiwan flooded the market with LCD panels. This contributed to a fall in LCD television prices in yen terms of 220% between January 2005 and December 2011 (see Figure 16).

The GFC accelerated after the collapse of Lehmann Brothers in September 2008. Television manufacturers had to offer steep discounts to induce consumers to spend (Waters, 2008). Consumers eschewed expensive 60-inch TVs (Kwong, 2012). One analyst noted that "Sharp spent about 430 billion yen on the largest LCD factory in the world ... perfectly suited to making 60, 70, and 80-inch TVs for outrageous prices that nobody wanted to buy. Koreans were making up to 50-inch TVs and undercutting the Japanese 50 per cent in the US market, the world's biggest."[18]

For the 2008 fiscal year, Sharp reported an operating loss of 55.5 billion yen. This was Sharp's first loss since the company was publicly listed in 1956. After generating profits over the next couple of years, it suffered operating losses of 545 billion yen in fiscal year (FY) 2012. It also reported material doubt about its ability to survive. Mizuho and Bank of Tokyo-Mitsubishi UFJ provided a debt-for-equity swap and Sharp laid off workers and cut costs. Sharp returned briefly to profitability but then lost 222 billion yen in FY2014 and again reported material doubt about its ability to survive. After losses in FY2015, Japanese banks insisted that Sharp be sold. Foxconn, a Taiwanese manufacturer, offered $4.4 billion in January 2016 and bought Sharp for $3.5 billion in March 2016.

---

[18] Birmingham (2013).

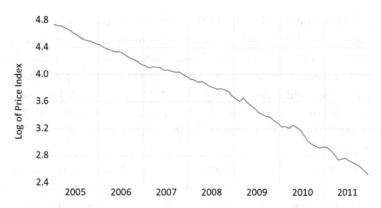

**Figure 16** Japanese consumer price index for LCD televisions
**Source:** Bank of Japan

Sony and Panasonic's television operations suffered similar humiliations. Sony was the world's leading TV producer until 2006. In 2009 it set a target of 40 million TV sales. In 2011 it reduced this target to 20 million (Soble, 2012). By 2012 its television division had lost money for eight years straight. Troubles selling televisions also caused Panasonic to lose $10 billion in FY2011 and to forecast similar losses in FY2012 (Soble, 2012).

While intense foreign competition and decreased demand during the GFC harmed Japanese television producers, the 45% yen appreciation against the dollar between July 1, 2007, and November 1, 2012, decimated them. Thorbecke (2012) found that the yen appreciation led to large falls in yen export prices for televisions. Given the intense competition in the TV market, Japanese exporters could not raise foreign currency prices when the yen strengthened. Instead, Thorbecke reported, the yen appreciation caused Japanese yen export prices for televisions to fall 31%. Yen costs of producing fell much more slowly than yen export prices, since it took time to move factories out of Japan. This collapse in yen revenues relative to yen costs decimated the profitability of Japanese television manufacturers.

The impact of the strong yen on the profitability of Japanese producers is evident in Figure 17. The figure shows the nominal yen/dollar exchange rate and stock prices for the Japanese consumer electronics industry and the overall Japanese stock market. The yen began appreciating on July 9, 2007, as concern about the GFC led to safe haven capital inflows into Japan. It appreciated 44% up to November 14, 2012. On that day Prime Minister Yoshihiko Noda called for a general election. The likely next prime minister, Shinzo Abe, called on November 14 for the Bank of Japan (BoJ) to print unlimited quantities of yen to raise inflation (Keohane, 2012). Anticipation of this policy caused the yen to

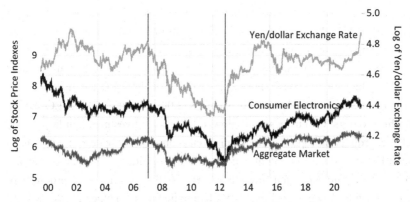

**Figure 17** Japanese consumer electronics stock prices, Japanese aggregate
stock prices, and the yen/dollar nominal exchange rate
**Source:** Datastream database

begin depreciating and the yen continued depreciating as Abe was elected and
the BoJ increased the quantity of yen.

Figure 17 shows that consumer electronics stocks fell by 200% between
July 9, 2007, and November 14, 2012. Then, beginning exactly on
November 15, they began increasing and continued increasing for the next
nine years. The moves in the consumer electronics stocks were more dramatic
than the moves in the overall Japanese stock market. Figure 17 shows that the
aggregate stock market fell 87% during the *endaka* period. The aggregate
market also appreciated more slowly than consumer electronics stocks over
the yen depreciation period after November 14.

While Japanese electronics firms were struggling, Samsung and LG stole
a march. Sato and colleagues (2013) reported that the Korean firms cut
production costs when the won was appreciating up until the end of 2007.
They then gained additional price competitiveness as the won depreciated
more than 50% against the dollar between November 2008 and March 2009.
When the won subsequently appreciated, they maintained competitiveness by
cutting costs further.

As flat panels are the costliest inputs to televisions, falling LCD prices led to
televisions becoming a commodity. Price wars broke out between Korean,
Japanese, and Chinese producers. Samsung and LG chose different paths to
avoid crippling competition (Jung-a, 2014). Samsung opted to make technologically advanced LCD panels and use these to produce ultra-high-definition TVs. LG
chose to make organic light-emitting diode (OLED) panels and use these to
produce televisions with better picture quality, lower power consumption, and
more flexible screens than LCD TVs. Speaking of their strategy, LG vice president

Oh Chang-ho said, "LCD has no future. The Chinese can make even ultra high-definition TVs at lower costs. We cannot win this price war. For survival, we have to make products that they cannot make."[19]

LG faced difficulties making large OLED panels. For this reason, the price of OLED televisions was high. For instance, the 55-inch OLED TV that LG began selling in America in March 2013 cost $12,000 (Nuttall, 2013). LG earned profits from its TV business and plowed these into investments in large-sized OLED production capacity. To benefit from economies of scale, it built plants in both Korea and China. It continued to iron out production problems, increase production efficiency, and lower costs. By 2019 it was the sole producer of large-sized OLED panels (Lex, 2019). It supplied these to other TV makers and used these to manufacture its own televisions. By 2022 LG's 55-inch OLED televisions cost less than $1,000.

China was concerned that its firms produced low-end goods and aimed to produce advanced goods (Patel, 2012). The Chinese government provided generous subsidies to develop flat-panel manufacturing (Hosokawa, 2020). Chinese LCD panel manufacturers such as BOE Technology Group depended on engineers and technicians from Japan and the United States to facilitate production (Ryugen, 2020). Between 2018 and 2019 Chinese firms increased their global market share of TFT LCDs from 3.6% to 33.9%. The flood of Chinese panels squeezed Korean and Taiwanese LCD manufacturers.

Samsung responded to the LCD price wars by announcing in 2019 that it would exit large LCD panel production. It planned to focus on what it called quantum-dot OLED displays, claiming that these would produce colors on TV screens that are close to natural colors. When the COVID-19 pandemic hit in 2020, consumer demand for televisions and other electronic products soared. Samsung thus delayed its exit from LCD manufacturing. In 2022 it brought its first quantum-dot OLED televisions to market.

## Mobile Phones

Before the iPhone was launched in 2007 several mobile phone makers competed. These included Nokia, Research in Motion (maker of the Blackberry), Samsung, Motorola, and other Japanese firms. Japanese firms such as Sharp, Panasonic, Fujitsu, NEC, Toshiba, and Sony Ericsson produced technologically advanced phones and focused on the Japanese market. Across the world, firms sold 825 million mobile phones in 2005 (Isaacson, 2011).

In 2007 Steve Jobs introduced the iPhone. Instead of employing a hardware keyboard like the Blackberry, he employed a touch-driven keyboard on the

---

[19] Quoted in Jung-a (2014).

screen controlled by software. Isaacson (2011) said that Jobs bet the company on the iPhone. While this revolutionary product threatened the high end of the mobile phone market, innovations by the Taiwanese chipmaker MediaTek challenged the low end. In 2006 MediaTek offered a turnkey solution to manufacture cellphones (Xing, 2021a). One chip package contained the hardware and software necessary to power a cellphone. Small firms in China with only 10 employees started using MediaTek's chip set to make budget phones. A few years later MediaTek developed chip packages to power smartphones.

In 2007 Google unveiled the Android operating system designed for smartphones. It was open source and freely available. It drastically lowered entry costs for firms wanting to produce phones.

The iPhone, the provision of free cellphone blueprints from MediaTek, and the launching of a free operating system from Google upended the industry. The iPhone became the highest-grossing phone. Free assembly information and software for cellphones and smartphones gave the advantage at the low end to companies with low-cost labor. The Android operating system made it hard for phone makers to differentiate their products.

This combination decimated the Japanese phone industry. MediaTek's free designs promoted modularization. Modularization allows firms to mix and match components to assemble a product (Xing, 2021a). It enables firms with weak technology and low labor costs to compete with advanced firms. Modularization destroyed the cellphone business of Sharp, Japan's leading phone producer (Yoshida, 2016). Other Japanese firms, skilled at craftsmanship and *monotsukuri* (making things), suffered in the digital, software-driven ecosystem.

Nokia was also destroyed. Competition at the high end from the iPhone and at the low end by producers using MediaTek's chips proved devastating. Stephen Elop left Microsoft to become CEO of Nokia in 2010. He sought to rejuvenate Nokia's struggling business. After presiding over the annihilation of Nokia's phone business, Elop left Nokia in 2014 with a 24.2 million euro payoff and returned to Microsoft. He also transferred the remains of Nokia's handset business to Microsoft (Milne, 2014).

While Sharp, Nokia, and other brands languished, Samsung and several Chinese phone makers prospered. By 2012 Samsung had become the largest phone manufacturer by sales. It continues to have the world's highest market share in 2022. Chinese firms began by honing their skills selling to third- and fourth-tier Chinese cities (Xing, 2021a). They then turned to more demanding markets. By 2022 four of the six brands with the highest market share in the world were Chinese – Xiaomi, Huawei, Oppo, and Vivo.

While Apple, Samsung, and the Chinese manufacturers are the dominant brands, many companies supply P&C. Japanese firms supply high-tech components that depend on craftsmanship. These include Murata, which produces sophisticated ceramic filters, and Sony, which makes image sensors. Korean and American firms supply dynamic random access memory and NAND flash memory. These include Samsung and Hynix from Korea and Micron Technology from the United States. Korean, Chinese, and Japanese firms supply panels. These include Samsung, BOE Technology, and JDI. China's role in the value chain has grown. Xing (2021a) reports that Chinese parts comprise 3.6% of the manufacturing costs of the iPhone 3G launched in 2008 but 25.4% of the costs of the iPhone X launched in 2018.

While Chinese parts suppliers have moved up the iPhone value chain, Chinese phone makers have increased value-added through establishing their own brands. Xing (2021b) documented that, for the phones released in 2017, Chinese firms contributed 16.7% of the manufacturing costs for Oppo smartphones and 15.4% of the costs for Xiaomi smartphones. However, since these Chinese brands also received the markup over costs, Chinese firms received 45.3% of the retail price of the Oppo phone and 41.7% of the retail price of the Xiaomi phone. Thus, while Oppo and Xiaomi relied on foreign technology, they captured much of the value-added by building their own brands. Xing (2021b) labels this approach of jumping to brand building before acquiring sufficient technology a nonlinear model of innovation.

While firms in many countries supply P&C, final assembly is performed largely in China and to a lesser extent in Vietnam. Figure 18 present phone exports from the four leading exporting countries. In 2018 the value of exports

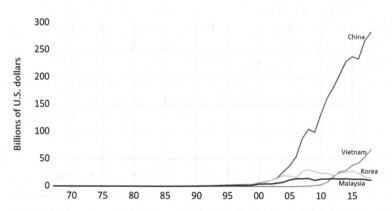

**Figure 18** Exports of cellphones and related items from the four leading exporters

**Note:** The figure presents exports from International Standard Industrial Classification Code 3220 (Manufacture of television and radio transmitters and apparatus for line telephony and line telegraphy).

**Source:** CEPII-CHELEM database

equaled almost $285 billion for China, $68 billion for Vietnam, $15 billion for Korea, and $11 billion for Malaysia. Companies such as Foxconn assemble phones for export in China. Samsung also takes advantage of cheaper labor in Vietnam to assemble phones.

Figure 18 shows that China has emerged as by far the largest exporter of phones. The same is true for other high-technology goods. As Xing (2021a) noted, China emerged as a leading exporter through a very different path than Japan and South Korea followed. Unlike firms in Japan and Korea, Chinese firms did not invent the advanced technology. Instead, they began by supplying lower value-added inputs to products being made by lead firms in global value chains (GVCs). As Xing discussed, for smartphones Chinese firms provided standardized parts such as batteries, antennas, and camera lens filters and low-skilled services such as testing and assembly. As demand for smartphones soared, demand for these Chinese inputs going into the phones also soared. Chinese firms also benefitted from producing for famous brands and taking advantage of their distribution and retail networks. While the fixed costs of promoting their own brands and establishing distribution and retail networks were prohibitive for many Chinese firms, they bypassed these obstacles by selling directly to lead firms in GVCs. Participating in these value chains thus contributed to China's export miracle.

## The Trade War and the Pandemic

As Figure 19 shows, China's exports to the United States have far exceeded China's imports from the United States year after year. The figure also indicates that China's exports to the United States and the gap between exports and imports exploded after China joined the WTO in 2001. Much of the surplus came from the electronics sector. If the surplus is corrected for US value-added in electronics, the surplus would shrink (Xing, 2021a). This is because high-tech US firms such as Apple, Qualcomm, and Micron Technology provide value-added to Chinese electronics exports. However, as the Stolper–Samuelson theorem predicts, China's trade liberalization in 2001 benefited capital in the United States (the abundant factor) and harmed labor (the scarce factor).

Few anticipated how much harm would come to US workers. Autor, Dorn, and Hanson (2013) reported that job losses in the United States after China joined the WTO occurred in industries most exposed to competition from China. Acemoglu, Autor, Dorn, Hanson, and Price (2014) and Pierce and Schott (2016) found that China's imports generated "stunning" losses in US manufacturing jobs. Pierce and Schott observed that many job losses were

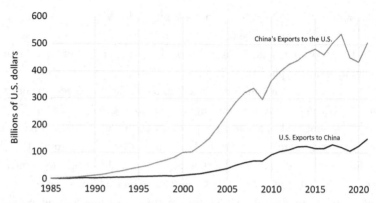

**Figure 19** China's exports to the United States and US exports to China
**Source:** US Census Bureau

concentrated in specific regions (e.g., the Southeast), making it harder for workers in the region to find new jobs. Case and Deaton (2015) reported a surge in deaths from suicide, drug abuse, or alcohol-related diseases in middle-aged whites without college degrees. Pierce and Schott found that more of these "deaths of despair" occurred in US counties exposed to imports from China.[20]

Workers' struggles led to protectionist pressure that boiled over with the election of Donald Trump to the presidency of the United States in 2016. Trump launched a trade war against China. The United States first imposed 25% tariffs on $50 billion of Chinese imports in June 2018. This included 25% tariffs on semiconductor imports. China retaliated with tariffs on $50 billion of US imports. The trade war escalated and average US tariffs on Chinese imports rose from 3.1% to 19.3%. Average Chinese tariffs on US imports rose from 8.0% to 20.7% (Bown, 2021). The United States applied tariffs on 66.4% of Chinese imports and China imposed tariffs on 58.3% of US imports.

The Trump administration also focused on perceived security threats from China. The Chinese company Huawei was seeking to build 5G networks abroad. The United States thought this could give the Chinese government access to sensitive data. As Bown (2021) recounted, the United States restricted exports to Huawei. Huawei, however, was able to import from Taiwan and South Korea. The United States then restricted sales to Huawei of any goods made abroad that used US technology. The United States also imposed restrictions on sales to the Chinese company Semiconductor Manufacture International Corporation.

---

[20] Feenstra and Sasahara (2018) documented that job gains from US exports to the world exceeded job losses from US imports from China.

Trump also sought to relocate electronics manufacturing to the United States. Foxconn, responding to threats from President Trump to impose tariffs on goods from China, told Trump that it would build an LCD manufacturing plant in Wisconsin. In 2017 it inked a deal with the State of Wisconsin to build a fab that could employ up to 13,000 people. Wisconsin in turn offered $3 billion in subsidies.

Foxconn never delivered on its agreement. According to Dzieza (2020), instead of building a 20 million-square-foot LCD fab, it built an empty building one-twentieth that size. Rather than providing work for 13,000 people, at the end of 2019 it employed only 281. Employees were hired with no actual work to do. Many were laid off after Foxconn received subsidies for hiring them.

Establishing an LCD fab in the United States is ill conceived (Hille, 2021). The United States does not possess locational advantages for LCD production. Manufacturing in the United States is costly. The United States also lacks the industrial clusters with supplier firms that provide inputs to LCD factories. The LCD industry faces cutthroat competition to make a commoditized product. Even with generous government subsidies, producing panels in the United States is uneconomical.

Figure 19 indicates that China's exports to the United States and its trade surplus began falling as the trade war emerged in 2018. However, Figure 4 indicates that East Asia's surplus with the United States kept increasing during the trade war. Firms avoided tariffs by relocating production to other Asian countries. For instance, Vietnam's exports to the United States increased from $42 billion in 2016 to $102 billion in 2021. Its trade surplus with the United States over this time increased from $32 billion to $91 billion.[21]

While the trade war buffeted the electronics industry, the COVID-19 pandemic arrived in 2020. Automakers and other industries cancelled their orders for chips. The pandemic caused semiconductor stocks beginning February 19, 2020, to fall by 30% in Taiwan, 38% in the United States, 41% in Korea, and 57% in Japan. However, as individuals worked and huddled at home, the demand for computers, phones, televisions, and other electronic equipment soared. Carmakers also saw demand increase as people eschewed public transportation. This produced a surge in demand for semiconductors. After reaching lows in March 2020, semiconductor stocks over the next year rose by 100% in Taiwan, 80% in the United States, 77% in Korea, and 104% in Japan.

A semiconductor shortage ensued. Automakers who had canceled orders for chips now could not obtain them. They had to shut down factories because they

---

[21] These data come from the US Census Bureau (www.census.gov).

could not obtain devices that cost only $2 (see, e.g., Jung-a, 2021). The semiconductor shortage highlighted the importance of this industry. Government officials realized how dependent their economies and their militaries are on chips. If semiconductors from East Asia became unavailable due to a natural disaster or war, the results would be catastrophic. The United States and other countries sought to relocate production domestically.

The Creating Helpful Incentives to Produce Semiconductors (CHIPS) for America Act was signed into law in August 2022. It allocates more than $50 billion to building US factories for semiconductor manufacturing, assembly, and testing and to R&D. Intel CEO Pat Gelsinger lobbied hard for the bill. In 2021 Gelsinger earned $179 million. In contrast, the CEO of Taiwan Semiconductor Manufacturing Company, the world's most successful semiconductor manufacturer, earned $447,000.

Gelsinger's compensation was calculated partly by Monte Carlo simulations forecasting how Intel's stock price was expected to perform (Waters, 2022). Gelsinger became CEO on February 15, 2021. By April 8, 2022, stock prices were 27% below their value when Gelsinger took over. Thus private investors are not optimistic about Intel's prospects, even given the likelihood of large government subsidies.

### *Thucydides's Trap and Escalating Conflict between China and the United States*

Allison (2017) argued that China and the United States face a Thucydides's Trap, a term that refers to the conflict that emerges when a rising power confronts a dominant one. In Thucydides's time, Athens was rising and Sparta was dominant. These two city-states ultimately fought in the Peloponnesian War. Allison noted that this trap risks ensnaring China and the United States. Allison documented 16 cases over the past 500 years when a rising power confronted a dominant one. Of these, 12 ended in war.

Relations between the United States and China are increasingly strained. Because electronic devices such as semiconductors can be used for both military and civilian purposes, the United States has imposed limitations on electronics exports to China. On October 7, 2022, President Biden imposed broad-ranging restrictions on China's ability to import and manufacture advanced chips. His goal was to limit China's ability to build advanced weapons, but the restrictions also hamper the development of China's civilian electronics industry.

Supply chains in Asia are bifurcating. Murata, a leading maker of electronic components, is developing one supply chain for the US-led economic bloc and one for the China-led bloc (Obe, 2022). Apple, after initially certifying NAND flash memory made by China's Yangtze Memory Technologies for use in its iPhones, relented under pressure from the US government (Lex, 2022).

The economic and especially the human costs of a war between the United States and China are unimaginable. Both sides should seek to reduce the tensions. One way would be to find areas where they can work together. Two possible areas are environmental protection and exchange rate cooperation. Another way would be to recognize how difficult communication is between East Asians and Americans and to take every step to communicate effectively. A shouting match between senior US and Chinese officials in Alaska in March 2021 was aggravated when the Chinese representatives did not understand the meaning of some of the English expressions that the American representatives used.

A third way would be for the United States to avoid unnecessarily provoking China. Many US politicians staged high-profile visits to Taiwan in 2022. These visits infuriated Chinese officials and provoked the Chinese military. If US and Taiwanese politicians wish to confer, they should do so out of the limelight or even in secret. A fourth would be for the grown-ups in the room in the United States and China to confer together. Confrontations between the United States and China resemble those between two boys squaring off on a playground. If cooler heads in the United States and China can exert influence, they can help their countries avoid war. The longer that the United States and China can maintain the status quo, the greater the chance that war can be avoided.

## Interpretation

The evolution of the television and mobile phone industries illustrates the slicing up of the value chain. Production blocks are allocated to different locations based on comparative advantage. The iPhone is designed in California, employs power management chips and other technology from Apple, OLED displays from Samsung, image sensors from Sony, ceramic filters from Murata, flash memory from Kioxia, and batteries from Sunwoda. It is then assembled by Foxxconn or Pegatron in China and a few other places. Apple in the United States has an advantage in design. Samsung produces OLED displays cheaply and efficiently. Japanese companies such as Sony, Murata, and Kioxia excel at producing differentiated products requiring craftsmanship. Chinese firms such as Sunwoda have advanced technologically and their parts comprise 25% of production costs. Foxconn then employs disciplined and affordable Chinese workers and the excellent Chinese infrastructure to assemble and ship iPhones.

Production of phones, televisions, and other electronic products within Asian value chains has been awesomely efficient. They involve both intense competition and intricate cooperation. They have caused Asia to become the manufacturing center for electronics and generated large gains to workers in Asia and losses to workers in the United States.

The travails of American workers led to a trade war with China. The trade war failed to reduce America's trade deficit with East Asia, but instead led to a relocation of production from China to other places such as Vietnam. The trade balance is a macroeconomic relationship, and, if the United States spends more than it saves, then tariffs will not correct its global trade deficit (see, e.g., Lawrence, 2022). Thus expenditure-switching policies such as tariffs or exchange rate appreciations are unlikely to be effective unless they are accompanied by expenditure-reducing policies such as cutting the US budget deficit.

The Japanese yen played a crucial role for Japanese electronics manufacturers. As Figure 17 shows, during the yen appreciation period from July 2007 to November 2012 consumer electronics stocks fell by 200%. Then, almost immediately after the yen started depreciating on November 14, 2012, these stocks began a rally that lasted nine years. Manufacturers largely followed a pricing-to-market strategy, so that the yen depreciation did not affect the volume of exports but rather the profitability of exporters (see, e.g., Thorbecke 2022).

Chinese firms developed a cutting edge flat-panel industry. To do this they depended on continued assistance from engineers and technicians from Japan, the United States, and other advanced countries. When foreign experts could no longer come during the COVID-19 pandemic, the Chinese panel industry suffered (Ryugen, 2020).

## 7 Lessons

*How Did Learning and Technological Progress Occur in East Asia?*

Keller (2021) noted that we know little about how learning by exporting occurs. The previous section considered how learning and technological progress occurred within the Asian electronics industry.

Japan after World War II was not allowed to produce military goods, so it focused on the consumer electronics market. The United States viewed free trade as a rampart against communism, so markets in the United States and elsewhere remained open. Entrepreneurs such as Akio Morita at Sony, Shoji Hattori at Seiko, and Tadashi Sasaki at Sharp envisioned products to satisfy consumer preferences. Because competition was cutthroat in the consumer electronics industry, firms faced incentives to master technologies in order to cut costs and differentiate their products.

Japan invested heavily in education at the time, with the number of engineering graduates per year increasing tenfold between 1940 and 1970. Engineers received not only technical training but also a broad liberal arts education. Engineers and entrepreneurs devoured the latest scientific journals and visited the United States to learn of the latest advances. Firms in the United States often sought lucrative defense contracts and did not view visitors from Japanese companies as competitors. They freely shared knowledge with their guests. The Japanese government–sponsored Electro-Technical Laboratory also proved invaluable to firms seeking technical knowledge.

Thus learning and technological progress in Japan occurred through a combination of factors. Researchers in the frontier country, the United States, were willing to share knowledge. The discipline of competition forced Japanese firms to pursue and assimilate appropriate technologies. Japanese engineers and researchers, being capable and well educated, were adept at absorbing technical knowledge and solving scientific problems. Entrepreneurs supplied vision and managers gave researchers freedom to dream. Researchers and factory workers were loyal to their firms and worked hard. This combination led to Japanese firms wowing consumers with Trinitron TVs, the Sony Walkman, camcorders, LCD watches, thin-screen TVs, and many other products.

Taiwan and South Korea, inspired by Japan's example, chose to compete in world markets. They also invested more in education than other economies at similar levels of development. In the 1960s and early 1970s their firms collaborated with Japanese firms. Japanese MNCs and trading companies (*sogo shosha*) provided technical assistance and training. The incentives of Japanese firms were aligned with those of Taiwanese and Korean firms. Japanese MNCs and trading companies wanted to ensure the quality of the goods they sold, and host country firms and workers wanted to acquire the knowledge and skills. In transferring production technology through the training of workers and managers, Japanese multinationals were following the model specified by Kojima (1973). By 1973 Taiwan was the third leading exporter of televisions.

In 1974 Taiwan confronted a perfect storm. It faced quotas on textile exports because of the Multi Fibre Arrangement. It had been forced to leave the United Nations. It severed relations with Japan and lost access to crucial Japanese capital goods and technology. Taiwan also suffered a 47% increase in consumer prices between 1972 and 1974 due to the first oil shock. In addition, it remained technically at war with mainland China.

Chinese researchers living abroad, Taiwanese government officials, and Taiwanese citizens pulled together to face the crisis. Eminent Chinese-American scientists and engineers recommended that Taiwan develop an IC industry. Taiwan purchased technology for design, process, manufacturing management and cost accounting from RCA. The government-sponsored ITRI oversaw the process and sent 40 engineers, several with US PhDs, to RCA for training. It then built a pilot IC plant and eventually spun off two world-class companies, UMC and TSMC.

Both UMC and TSMC are located in the government-established HSBIP. Two universities, National Tsing Hua University and National Chiao Tung University, are located nearby. The government also encouraged many engineers and researchers from the United States to return to Taiwan. The returnees not only brought back advanced technologies but also retained communication channels with Silicon Valley. They could call colleagues in the Valley to help resolve technical difficulties. As they interacted with engineers and researchers at HSBIP, ITRI, National Tsing Hua University, and National Chiao Tung University, technical knowledge spread throughout the cluster.

South Korea in the 1960s and 1970s faced the threat of invasion from the north. It viewed exports and economic development as essential in order to import military hardware, resources, and capital goods. The government directed banks to allocate working capital at below-market interest rates to firms. If the firms succeeded at exporting, banks continued to provide financing and if not they rescinded the credit. Most of the firms initially receiving subsidized loans initially no longer received them a decade later.

Samsung took the government's export incentives seriously. No foreign firms would sell color picture tubes to Samsung because it lacked the technology to make color TVs. Samsung then took apart foreign color TVs to learn how to make them. Within a few years it was exporting color TVs. It thus responded to the government's imperative by performing its own R&D and mastering new production techniques.

Korean workers were patriotic and determined to make Korea an economic giant. Samsung established a research institute in the United States where Korean engineers trained in the United States taught Samsung engineers. The Samsung engineers diligently learned from their teachers. They then worked day and night in Korea and soon produced chips that surpassed those made by their mentors.

Taiwan and Korea had several factors in common that contributed to learning and technological progress. Both faced serious threats, including to national security. Both viewed economic development as crucial for survival. Government officials, managers, workers, and citizens living abroad worked together to achieve development. Both economies also invested heavily in education, helping workers absorb new technologies. Their firms also sold in world markets and the discipline of competition forced them to master appropriate technologies.

Competition also drove innovation in Southeast Asian countries. Seagate in Thailand provided several weeks of training in the Thai language to its employees. It also established research links with and received technicians from the Asian Institute of Technology. When competition with other HDD manufacturers intensified, engineers at Seagate implemented process innovations. For example, they formed teams to analyze production defects. Each team was assigned one production process and when yields fell below 98% they stopped the production line to analyze the problem. They soon raised yields to 99.5–99.6%. Similarly, intense competition between firms supplying MNCs in Malaysia led them to introduce automation, statistical quality control, and JIT inventory practices.

Cooperation also created learning opportunities. In Thailand, employees of HDD makers and employees of their suppliers met daily to discuss production efficiency, cost savings, and possible changes. They coordinated production schedules, evaluated performance, and considered how to improve quality. Manufacturers and their suppliers always had to be ready to engage in R&D and innovate in response to new product cycles and unexpected changes in demand.

Exchange rates matter for exporting and thus learning, but within global value chains the link is more complicated than with traditional trade. China's exports soared in the twenty-first century and the value of the renminbi contributed to this. However, the value of the Japanese yen, New Taiwan dollar, and Korean won also mattered. Thorbecke (2019) found that, even as the renminbi appreciated, exchange rates in upstream Asian supply chain countries depreciated. This allowed Chinese exporters to maintain their price competitiveness and their export volumes.

Competition drove innovation in the flat-panel display industry after the GFC. Liquid crystal display panels and televisions made using them became commoditized. A brutal price war broke out between Asian producers. LG realized that, in order to survive, it needed to master technologies that its competitors lacked. It developed OLED panels to construct 55-inch televisions. In 2013 these TVs cost $13,000. By 2022 LG had improved productivity and the televisions cost less than $1,000.

## Lessons for the United States

The trade war and the COVID-19 pandemic have stimulated calls to relocate manufacturing to the United States. For instance, locating so much semiconductor manufacturing in Taiwan and South Korea multiplies risks to the US economy and national defense. If natural disasters, wars, or other factors interrupt the flow of these goods to America, US factories would stop producing and tanks, fighter jets, and aircraft carriers. Examining the path that East Asia took to build a strong electronics industry offers lessons for the United States.

Entrepreneurs drove much of Asia's success. Tadashi Sasaki at Sharp, Byung-Chull Lee at Samsung, Akio Morita at Sony, and many others were visionary leaders. They took risks with no guarantee of return. If their firms did not satisfy consumer preferences, then their companies would cease to exist and they would lose their jobs. In addition, in the case of Korea, if firms failed to meet the government's export targets they would lose their benefits and go bankrupt. Thus Asian entrepreneurs had powerful incentives to choose appropriate technologies, invest wisely, and produce efficiently.

Western CEOs in the electronics industry are rewarded whether or not their risks pay off. Nokia CEO Stephen Elop presided over the annihilation of Nokia and left with a 24.2 million euro payoff. Intel CEO Pat Gelsinger earned $179 million in his first year at Intel even as the company's stock price tumbled.

The US government is intent on subsidizing this business model. With the CHIPS for America Act, it is seeking to provide $50 billion to build US factories for semiconductor manufacturing. Intel would be the prime beneficiary of this largesse. There should be no surprise if $50 billion does not produce the desired results when entrepreneurs' incentives are not appropriately aligned with those of the government

Government attempts to establish LCD manufacturing in Wisconsin were disastrous.[22] They spent $400 million and employed eminent domain to force many to leave their homes in order to help Foxconn build a factory. They promised to spend billions of dollars more and Foxconn planned to hire more than 10,000 people. The cost per job of this subsidy would have been between $200,000 and $1 million. In the end fewer than 300 people worked there, and many spent their time watching Netflix and playing video games. High labor costs and the absence of supplier companies such as Corning Glass nearby made plans to establish an LCD factory in Wisconsin unrealistic. Billions of dollars in subsidies were not enough to rescue this foolhardy plan.

Hufbauer and Jung (2021) studied 18 US industrial policy episodes over the 1970–2020 period. They found that protectionist policies and benefits to a single firm typically failed. They reported that R&D subsidies can work when they are allocated by scientists and engineers free from political interference. They found that the best policies encouraged competition. For instance,

---

[22] This paragraph draws on Dzieza (2020).

Operation Warp Speed provided funding for COVID-19 vaccine research but also encouraged competition.

A lesson from industrial policy in Asia is that it works best when agents are united in fighting for the survival of the nation. Willett (1995) highlighted that, when national security concerns become paramount, the polity reacts as a unified actor. Agents in the political arena take actions for the good of the nation. At other times, interest group competition, rent-seeking, and distributional struggles can predominate. In South Korea and Taiwan, the threat of invasion was real. Economic development was seen as a way to promote national survival. Workers, entrepreneurs, government officials, and others worked together to achieve economic growth. In Malaysia, on the other hand, there was no threat to survival and redistributional policies abounded. Industrial policy in this environment did not succeed as it had in South Korea and Taiwan.

Rent-seeking is prevalent in the United States. The US company Boeing, after a series of manufacturing disasters in commercial jet manufacturing, is moving its headquarters from Chicago to Arlington, Virginia. The new headquarters is close to the Pentagon and Congress. Boeing already has 100 lobbyists in Washington, DC. Many interpret this move as a further refocus away from commercial manufacturing to lobbying for defense and space contracts (see, e.g., Isidore, 2022).

Previous sections documented how, while US scientists developed breakthrough technologies such as C-MOS chips and LCDs, Asian and not American firms profited from these. Asian firms faced the discipline of market competition. Asian companies had to choose technologies carefully and cut costs. American electronics firms, on the other hand, chased lucrative defense contracts. They devoted resources to lobbying government officials instead of satisfying consumer preferences. By changing companies' incentive structure, massive defense spending contributed to the offshoring of electronics manufacturing. Defense spending that relocated so much production to Asia actually weakened US national security.

Japan, South Korea, and Taiwan have historically run disciplined fiscal policies. Private saving rates were also high when the electronics industry emerged. This provided savings to meet the heavy investment requirements of the industry. The United States, by contrast, has run budget deficits averaging 4.5% of GDP between 2000 and 2021. Net saving as a percent of GDP (which includes government, business, and personal savings) has averaged 2.5% of GDP. Unsurprising, large budget deficits and low national saving rates have been associated with CAD. The United States' current account deficit has averaged 3.5% of GDP between 2000 and 2021. American indebtedness to the rest of the world grew from 58% in 2003 to 97% of GDP in 2021. The US external indebtedness at the end of 2021 almost exactly equaled US federal debt held by the public (99.6% of GDP). Thus the United States has gone heavily in debt over the past 20 years by borrowing from the rest of the world.[23]

Like an overweight patient should voluntarily go on a diet before suffering a heart attack, the United States should rebalance its economy before it is forced to. Fiscal discipline is necessary. In addition, a US dollar depreciation against the Japanese yen, the Korean won, the New Taiwan dollar, the Chinese renminbi, and other currencies together would help rebalance trade.

A concerted appreciation would also be in the interest of East Asian economies. They prospered through free trade with the United States. Persistent imbalances with America will multiply protectionist pressures in the United States. Also, by appreciating together, Japan, South Korea, Taiwan, and China will not lose price competitiveness relative to each other. Appreciations will increase the purchasing power of Asian consumers and firms. Finally, appreciations will help cool inflationary pressures and make commodities such as oil that are priced in dollars more affordable in Asia.

Analysts may object that Asian currencies can only appreciate when fundamentals drive it. Their current account surpluses and trade surpluses with the United States are a fundamental factor that can lead to appreciations against the US dollar. In addition, one should never underestimate the resourcefulness of Asian policy makers. They possess many instruments that they can use when it benefits their countries. For instance, government pension funds invest huge amounts overseas. If they invested more domestically or in nearby economies, Asian currencies would appreciate.

Another lesson from Asia for the United States is to provide quality education. This enables scientists to innovate, engineers to master new technologies, and factory workers to be productive. In the last Programme for International Student Assessment (PISA) tests measuring 15-year-olds' ability to use reading, mathematics, and science to meet real-life challenges, the rankings were: China 1st, Singapore 2nd, Macao 3rd, Hong Kong 4th, Japan 6th, Korea 7th, Taiwan 8th, and the United States 25th.[24] Improving educational outcomes in the United States should be a priority.

Hufbauer and Jung (2021) noted that competition is an American strength. The US government should remember this. The discipline of competing in

---

[23] Data on US budget deficits, net saving, CAD, and GDP are available at https://fred
.stlouisfed.org. Data on US indebtedness to the rest of the world are available at https://home
.treasury.gov/data/treasury-international-capital-tic-system. Data on US debt relative to GDP
are available at www.cbo.gov.

[24] Data and information on PISA are available at www.oecd.org/pisa.

global markets drove much of the innovation in the Asian electronics industry. In contrast, being coddled by the defense industry weakened American electronics manufacturing. Asia's experience also shows that manufacturing growth occurs when entrepreneurs face appropriate incentives, fiscal policy is disciplined, exchange rates are not too strong, education is emphasized, and industrial clusters emerge. To reshore electronics manufacturing, the United States should take a page from Asia's playbook.

The United States should also be modest in its goals.[25] Steve Jobs told President Obama in 2011 that Apple had 700,000 employees in China working under the supervision of 30,000 engineers. Jobs could not find that many engineers to work for him in the United States. The shortage of engineers in the United States is even greater now. If the United States cannot relocate sufficient production to America, it should consider "friendshoring" some to Ireland, India, and other allied countries.

---

[25] I am indebted to an anonymous referee for this suggestion.

# References

Acemoglu, D., Autor, D., Dorn, D., Hanson, G. & Price, B. (2014). Import competition and the great US employment saga of the 2000s. NBER Working Paper No. 20395. Cambridge, MA: National Bureau of Economic Research.

Acharya, R. & Keller, W. (2009). Technology transfer through imports. *Canadian Journal of Economics*, **42**(4), 1411–1448.

Ahmed, S. (2009). Are Chinese exports sensitive to changes in the exchange rate? International Finance Discussion Papers No. 987. Washington, DC: Federal Reserve Board.

Aitken, B. & Harrison, A. (1999). Do domestic firms benefit from direct foreign investment? Evidence from Venezuela. *American Economic Review*, **89**(3), 605–618.

Akamatsu, K. (1962). A historical pattern of economic growth in developing countries. *Developing Economies*, **1**(1), 3–25.

Akcigit, U. & Melitz, M. (2021). International trade and innovation. NBER Working Paper No. 29611. Cambridge, MA: National Bureau of Economic Research.

Allison, G. (2017). *Destined for War: Can America and China Escape the Thuydides's Trap?* New York: Houghton Mifflin Harcourt.

Aspray, W. (1994). Interview of Tadashi Sasaki. https://ethw.org/Oral-History: Tadashi_Sasaki.

Autor, D., Dorn, D. & Hanson, G. (2013). The China syndrome: Local labor market effects on import competition in the United States. *American Economic Review*, **103**(6), 2121–2168.

Bhagwati, J. (1988). *Protectionism*. Cambridge, MA: MIT Press.

Bhagwati, J. (1999). The "miracle" that did happen: Understanding East Asia in comparative perspective. In E. Thorbecke & H. Wan, eds., *Taiwan's Development Experience: Lessons on Roles of Government and Market.* Dordrecht: Kluwer Academic, pp. 21–39.

Birmingham, L. (2013). Electronics: Lifelines thrown to alleviate distress. *Financial Times*. March 28.

Bloom, N., Draca, M. & Van Reenen, J. (2016). Trade induced technical change? The impact of Chinese imports on innovation, IT and productivity. *Review of Economic Studies*, **83**(1), 87–117.

Bown, C. (2021). The US–China trade war and phase one agreement. *Journal of Policy Modeling*, **43**(4), 805–843.

Breznitz, D. (2007). *Innovation and the State: Political Choice and Strategies for Growth in Israel, Taiwan, and Ireland*. New Haven, CT: Yale University Press.

Brooks, D. (2000). Interview with Donald Brooks. February 8. Silicon Genesis: Oral history interviews of Silicon Valley scientists, 1995–2018. https://purl.stanford.edu/cj789gh7170.

Carmody, T. (2011). Without Jobs as CEO, who speaks for the arts at Apple? *Wired*. August 29.

Case, A. & Deaton, A. (2015). Rising morbidity and mortality in midlife among white non-Hispanic Americans in the 21st century. *Proceedings of the National Academy of Sciences*, **112**(49), 15078–15083.

Chai, Y. & Im, O. (2009). The development of free industrial zones: The Malaysian experience. Mimeo. World Bank. https://cpb-us-e1.wpmucdn.com/share.nanjing-school.com/dist/1/43/files/2012/10/info.worldbank.org-s9hsat.pdf.

Chang, P., Hsu, C. & Tsai, C. (1999). A stage approach for industrial technology development and implementation: The case of Taiwan's computer industry. *Technovation*, **19**(4), 233–241.

Chang, P., Shih, C. & Hsu, C. (1994). The formation process of Taiwan's IC industry: Method of technology transfer. *Technovation*, **14**(3), 161–171.

Chang, P. & Tsai, C. (2002). Finding the niche position: Competition strategy of Taiwan's IC design industry. *Technovation*, **22**(2), 101–111.

Chang, S. (2008). *Sony vs Samsung: The Inside Story of the Electronics Giants' Battle for Global Supremacy*. Hoboken, NJ: Wiley.

Chen, T. & Ku, Y. (2000). The effect of foreign direct investment on firm growth: The case of Taiwan's manufacturers. *Japan and the World Economy*, **12**(2),153–172.

Dedrick, J., Kraemer, K. & Linden, G. (2010). Who profits from innovation in global value chains? A study of the iPod and notebook PCs. *Industrial and Corporate Change*, **19**(1), 81–116.

Dee, P. (1984). Economic policy making and the role of special interest groups: Some evidence for South Korea. Kiel Working Paper No. 217. Kiel, Germany: Kiel Institute for the World Economy.

De Loecker, J. (2007). Do exports generate higher productivity? Evidence from Slovenia. *Journal of International Economics*, **73**(1), 69–98.

Destler, I. (1986). *American Trade Politics: System under Stress*. Washington, DC: Institute for International Economics.

Dosi, G., Virgillito, E. & Yu, X. (2020). The wage-productivity nexus in the world factory Economy. *World Development*, **129**, Article 104875.

Dzieza, J. (2020). The eighth wonder of the world. *The Verge*. October 19.

Feenstra, R. & Sasahara, A. (2018). The China shock, exports and US employment: A global input-output analysis. *Review of International Economics*, **26**(5), 1053–1083.

Freund, C. & Moran, T. (2017). Multi-national investors as export superstars: How emerging-market governments can reshape comparative advantage. Working Paper No. 17–1. Washington, DC: Peterson Institute for International Economics.

Garcia-Marin, A. & Voigtländer, N. (2019). Exporting and plant-level efficiency gains: It's in the measure. *Journal of Political Economy*, **127**(4), 1777–1825.

Harding, R. (2008). Sony fights to regain technological edge. *Financial Times*. December 10.

Harding, R. & Kwong, R. (2009). Why the plug was pulled on plasma. *Financial Times*. February 13.

Hattori, T. & Sato, Y. (1997). A comparative study of development mechanisms in Korea and Taiwan: Introductory analysis. *Developing Economies*, **35**(4), 341–357.

Hausmann, R. (2013). The tacit-knowledge economy. Project-Syndicate Weblog. October 30. www.project-syndicate.org.

Hausmann, R. (2021). Lack of progress cannot be solved by a redistributive strategy. In I. Goldfajn & E. Levy Yeyati, eds., *Latin America: The Post-pandemic Decade*. London: CEPR Press, pp. 75–87.

Hausmann, R., Hidalgo, C., Bustos, S. et al., Coscia, M., Simoes, A., and Yıldırım, M. (2013). The Atlas of Economic Complexity., Cambridge, MA: The MIT Press.

Hausmann, R., Hidalgo, C., Bustos, S. et al. (2013). *The Atlas of Economic Complexity*. Cambridge, MA: MIT Press.

Hausmann, R. & Neffke, F. (2019). The workforce of pioneer plants: The role of worker mobility in the diffusion of industries. *Research Policy*, **48**(3), 628–648.

Hausmann, R. & Rodrik, D. (2003). Economic development as self-discovery. *Journal of Development Economics*, **72**(2), 603–633.

Hayami, Y. & Goto, Y. (2011). The role of education in the economic catch-up: Comparative growth experiences from Japan, Korea, Taiwan, and the United States. In K. Hamada, ed., *Miraculous Growth and Stagnation in Post-war Japan*. London: Routledge, pp. 112–134.

Hayter, R. & Edgington, D. (2004). Flying geese in Asia: The impacts of Japanese MNCs as a source of industrial learning. *Journal of Economic and Human Geography*, **95**(1), 3–26.

Hille, K. (2021). Tale of Taiwan's tech giants in US reveals divide in approach. *Financial Times*. May 18.

Hiratsuka, D. (2011). Production networks in Asia: A case study from the hard disk drive industry. ADBI Working Paper No. 301. Tokyo: Asian Development Bank Institute.

Hobday, M. (1995a). East Asian latecomer firms: Learning the technology of electronics. *World Development*, **23**(7), 1171–1193.

Hobday, M. (1995b). Innovation in East Asia: Diversity and development. *Technovation*, **15**(2), 55–63.

Hobday, M., Cawson, A. & Kim, S. (2001). Governance of technology in the electronics industries of East and South-East Asia. *Technovation*, **21**(4), 209–226.

Hobday, M. & Rush, H. (2007). Upgrading the technological capabilities of foreign transnational subsidiaries in developing countries: The case of electronics in Thailand. *Research Policy*, **36**(9), 1335–1356.

Hosokawa, K. (2020). LG and Samsung in full retreat before Chinese flat-panel onslaught. *Financial Times*. April 29.

Hufbauer, G. & Jung, E. (2021). Lessons learned from half a century of US industrial policy. Realtime Economic Issues Watch. Washington DC: Peterson Institute for International Economics.

Ikeda, D. & Morita, Y. (2020). The effects of barriers to technology adoption on japanese prewar and postwar economic growth. *Journal of the Japanese and International Economies*, 55, 101061.

Inada, M. & Guo, Y. (2016). Heterogeneous impacts of a change in Chinese FDI regulations on domestic market outcomes: Empirical evidence from Taiwanese plant data. Discussion Paper 934. Kyoto, Japan: Kyoto Institute of Economic Research.

International Monetary Fund (IMF). (2007). *Exchange Rates and the Adjustment of External Imbalances: World Economic Outlook Chapter 3*. Washington, DC: International Monetary Fund.

Irwin, D. (1996). The U.S.–Japan semiconductor trade conflict. In A. Krueger, ed., *The Political Economy of Trade Protection*. Chicago: University of Chicago Press, pp. 5–13.

Isaacson, W. (2011). *Steve Jobs*. New York: Simon & Schuster.

Isidore, C. (2022). Boeing is losing the plane race. So it packed up and left for Washington. *CNN Business*. May 9.

Johnstone, B. (1999). *We Were Burning: Japanese Entrepreneurs and the Forging of the Electronic Age*. New York: Basic Books.

Jones, R. & Kierzkowski, H. (1990). The role of services in production and international trade: A theoretical framework. In R. Jones & A. Krueger, eds., *The Political Economy of International Trade*. Oxford: Blackwell, pp. 31–48.

Jung-a, S. (2014). LG display on mission to reshape flexible screens. *Financial Times*. July 22.

Jung-a, S. (2021). Hyundai faces production hit from April as chip shortage bites. *Financial Times*. March 24.

Kahney, L (2004). Inside look at birth of the iPod. *Wired*. July 21.

Karimi, M. & Yusop, Z. (2009). FDI and economic growth in Malaysia. Mimeo. University Putra Malaysia. https://mpra.ub.uni-muenchen.de/14999/1/MPRA_paper_14999.pdf.

Kawakami, M. (1996). *Development of the Small- and Medium-Sized Manufacturers in Taiwan's PC Industry*. Tapei: Chung-Hua Institute for Economic Research.

Keller, W. (2021). Knowledge spillovers, trade, and FDI. NBER Working Paper No. 28739. Cambridge, MA: National Bureau of Economic Research.

Kelly, L. (2017). 5 companies that have shaped Asia, and the world. *Forbes*. September 20.

Keohane, D. (2012). Tokyo political turmoil hits yen. *Financial Times*. November 15.

Kim, L. (1980). Stages of development of industrial technology in a LDC: A model. *Research Policy* 9(3), 254–277.

Kim, L. & Dahlman, C. (1992). Technology policy for industrialization: An integrative framework and Korea's experience. *Research Policy*, 21(5), 437–452.

Kimura, F. & Ando, M. (2005). Two-dimensional fragmentation in East Asia: Conceptual framework and empirics. *International Review of Economics & Finance*, 14(3), 317–348.

Kiyota, K., Urata, S., Matsuura, T. & Wei, Y. (2008). Reconsidering the backward vertical linkages of foreign affiliates: Evidence from Japanese multinationals. *World Development*, 36(8), 238–250.

Kohpaiboon, A. & Poapongsakorn, N. (2011). Industrial upgrading and global recession: Evidence of hard disk drive and automotive industries in Thailand. ADBI Working Paper No. 283. Tokyo: Asian Development Bank Institute.

Kojima, K. (1973). A macroeconomic approach to foreign direct investment. *Hitotsubashi Journal of Economics*, 14(1), 1–21.

Kraemer, K., Linden, G. & Dedrick, J. 2011. Capturing value in global networks: Apple's iPad and iPhone. Mimeo. University of California, Irvine. http://econo miadeservicos.com/wp-content/uploads/2017/04/value_ipad_iphone.pdf.

Krueger, A. (1997). Trade policy and economic development: How we learn. NBER Working Paper No. 5896. Cambridge, MA: National Bureau of Economic Research.

Kwong, R. (2012). Japan losing edge over Korea and Taiwan. *Financial Times*. April 11.

Lawrence, R. (2022). Looking at all the wrong places to reduce the US trade deficit. Realtime Economic Issues Watch. Washington, DC: Peterson Institute for International Economics.

Lee, J. & Wie, D. (2015). Technological change, skill demand, and wage inequality: Evidence from Indonesia. *World Development*, **67**, 238–250.

Lex. (2019). Samsung: Always on display. *Financial Times*. October 10.

Lex. (2022). Apple/China: Suspending plan to use Yangtze chips means more local tech problems. *Financial Times*. October 17.

Lin, Y. & Rasiah, R. (2014). Human capital flows in Taiwan's technological catch up in integrated circuit manufacturing. *Journal of Contemporary Asia*, **44**(1), 64–83.

Liu, C. (1993). Government's role in developing a high-tech industry: The case of Taiwan's semiconductor industry. *Technovation*, **13**(5), 299–309.

Milne, R. (2014). Stephen Elop gets bigger-than-expected €24.2m Nokia payoff. *Financial Times*. May 1.

Modi, A. (1989). Strategies for developing information industries. *European Journal of Development Research*, **1**(1), 38–59.

Mundell, R. A. (1957). International trade and factor mobility. *American Economic Review*, **47**(3), 321–335.

Nurkse, R. (1953). *Problems of Capital Formation in Underdeveloped Countries*. Oxford: Basil Blackwell.

Nurkse, R. (1959). *Patterns of Trade and Development, Wicksell Lectures*. Stockholm: Almquist and Wicksell.

Nuttall, C. (2013). CESsentials 2013: LG gets smarter with TVs. *Financial Times*. January 8.

Obe, M. (2022). Japan tech supplier Murata warns over rapid U.S.–China decoupling. *Nikkei Asia*. October 18.

Ohkawa, K. & Kohama, H. (1989). *Lectures on Developing Economies: Japan's Experience and Its Relevance*. Tokyo: University of Tokyo Press.

Ohkawa, K. & Rosovsky, H. (1973). *Japanese Economic Growth: Trend Acceleration in the Twentieth Century*. Stanford, CA: Stanford University Press.

Ohno, K. (2017). *The History of Japanese Economic Development*. London: Routledge.

Okimoto, D., Sugano, T. & Weinstein, F. (1984). *Competitive Edge: The Semiconductor Industry in the U.S. and Japan*. Stanford, CA: Stanford University Press.

Ozawa, T. (2007). Professor Kiyoshi Kojima's contributions to FDI theory: Trade, structural transformation, growth, and integration in East Asia. *International Economy*, **11**(1), 17–33.

Patel, K. (2012). China to Japan: Our TVs are bigger. *Financial Times*. March 13.

Patterson, A. (2007). Oral history of Morris Chang. CHM reference number X4151.2008, Computer History Museum.

Pecht, M., Bernstein, J., Searls, D., Pecherar, M. & Karulkar, P. (1997). *The Korean Electronics Industry*. London: Routledge.

Pierce, J. & Schott, P. (2016). The surprisingly swift decline of U.S. manufacturing employment. *American Economic Review*, **106**(7), 1632–1662.

Rasiah, R. (1999a). Regional dynamics and production networks: The development of electronics clusters in Malaysia. Mimeo. Universiti Malaysia Sarawak. www.researchgate.net/publication/237325427_REGIONAL_DYNAMICS_AND_PRODUCTION_NETWORKS_THE_DEVELO PMENT_OF_ELECTRONICS_CLUSTERS_IN_MALAYSIA.

Rasiah, R. (1999b). Malaysia's national innovation system. In G. Felker & K. S. Jomo, eds., *Technology, Competitiveness and the State: Malaysia's Industrial Technology Policies*. London: Routledge, pp. 180–198.

Rasiah, R. (2003). Foreign ownership, technology and electronics exports from Malaysia and Thailand. *Journal of Asian Economics*, **14**(5), 785–811.

Rasiah, R. (2010). Catch up in integrated circuits production: Malaysia compared to Korea and Taiwan. Inaugural Public Lecture of the Malaysian Centre of Regulatory Studies, University of Malaya, October 13.

Rasiah, R. (2017). The industrial policy experience of the electronics industry in Malaysia. In J. Page and F. Tarp, eds., *The Practice of Industrial Policy: Government-Business Coordination in Africa and East Asia*. Oxford: Oxford University Press, pp. 1–25.

Rodrik, D. (2008). The real exchange rate and economic growth. *Brookings Papers on Economic Activity*, Fall, 365–412.

Romer, P. (1990). Endogenous technological change. *Journal of Political Economy*, **98**(5), S71–S102.

Royal, W. (2004). Made in Taiwan. *Industry Week*. December 22.

Ryugen, H. (2020). China's factories struggle without key import: Foreign talent. *Financial Times*. April 28.

Samsung (2012). *The History of Samsung Electronics*. Seoul: Samsung Newsroom.

Sanchanta, M. (2007). Sharp to invest in 10th-generation LCD plant. *Financial Times*. August 1.

Sato, K., Shimizu, J., Shrestha, N. & Zhang, S. (2013). Industry-specific real effective exchange rates and export price competitiveness: The cases of Japan, China, and Korea. *Asia Economic Policy Review*, **8**(2), 298–321.

Sato, Y. (1997). Diverging development paths of the electronics industry in Korea and Japan. *Developing Economies*, **35**(4), 401–421.

Sawa, T. (2013). Lack of liberal arts education is sapping Japan's creativity. *Japan Times*. September 16.

Sherman, E. (2002). Inside the Apple iPod triumph design. *Electronics Design Chain*, Summer.

Soble, J. (2012). Sharp power shift in Asia tech industry. *Financial Times*. April 9.

Thangavelu, S. & Venkatachalam, A. (2020). Economic shocks and uncertainties: How does firm innovativeness enable supply chain and moderate interdependence? In A.Venkatachalam, F. Kimura & S. Thangavelu, eds., *Supply Chain Resilience: Reducing Vulnerability to Economic Shocks, Financial Crises, and Natural Disasters*. New York: Springer, pp. 15–36.

*The Star*. (2014). Globetronics: R&D Collaboration Yields Little Result. November 5. www.thestar.com.

Thorbecke, W. (2012). The short and long run effects of exchange rate changes on the Japanese electronics industry. RIETI Discussion Paper No. 12-E-019. Tokyo: Research Institute of Economy, Trade and Industry.

Thorbecke, W. (2017). Rebalancing trade in East Asia: Evidence from the electronics industry. *Emerging Markets Finance and Trade*, **53**(12), 2696–2705.

Thorbecke, W. (2019). East Asian value chains, exchange rates, and regional exchange rate arrangements. *Journal of Asian Economics*, **65**, Article 101132.

Thorbecke, W. (2022). Investigating how exchange rates affected the Japanese economy after the advent of Abenomics. *Asia and the Global Economy*, **2**(1), Article 100028.

Thorbecke, W. & Salike, N. (2014). FDI in East Asia: The role of production networks. In S. Tong, ed., *Trade, Investment, and Economic Integration*. Singapore: World Scientific, pp. 67–90.

Thorbecke, W. & Smith, G. (2010). How would an appreciation of the RMB and other East Asian currencies affect China's exports? *Review of International Economics*, **18**(1), 95–108.

Tomizawa, R. (2019). *1964. The Greatest Year in the History of Japan: How the Tokyo Olympics Symbolized Japan's Miraculous Rise from the Ashes*. Austin, TX: Liongate.

Tsou, M., Liu, J., Hammitt, J. & Chang, C. (2013). The impact of foreign direct investment in China on employment adjustments in Taiwan: Evidence from matched employer–employee data. *Japan and the World Economy*, **25–26**, 68–79.

Tuan, C. & Ng, L. (2004). Manufacturing agglomeration as incentives to Asian FDI in China after WTO. *Journal of Asian Economics*, **15**(4), 673–693.

Van Agtmael, A. (2007). *The Emerging Markets Century.* New York: Free Press.

Van Biesebroeck, J. (2005). Exporting raises productivity in sub-Saharan African manufacturing firms. *Journal of International Economics,* **67**(2), 373–391.

Wagner, R. (1993). *Parchment, Guns and Constitutional Order.* Cheltenham: Edward Elgar.

Waters, R. (2008). Electronics bargains spell trouble for tech industry. *Financial Times.* November 20.

Waters, R. (2022). Intel's stock award to lure Patrick Gelsinger as chief was worth $169.5 mn. *Financial Times.* March 31.

Willett, T. (1995). The public choice approach to international economic relations. Eleventh annual lecture in the Virginia Political Economy Lecture Series. Fairfax, Virginia, March 15.

Xing, Y. (2021a). *Decoding China's Export Miracle: A Global Value Chain Analysis.* Singapore: World Scientific.

Xing, Y. (2021b). Global value chains and the innovation of Chinese mobile phone industry. In E. Baak, B. Hofman & J. Qian, eds., *Innovation and China's Global Emergence.* Singapore: NUS Press, 263–286.

Yamashita, N. & Jayasuriya, S. (2013). The export response to exchange rates and product fragmentation: The case of Chinese manufactured exports. *Journal of the Asia Pacific Economy,* **18**(2), 318–332.

Yoshida, R. (2016). How modularization felled Japan's electronics titans. *Japan Times.* March 31.

Yoshitomi, M. (2003). *Post Crisis Development Paradigms in Asia.* Tokyo: Asian Development Bank Institute.

Yoshitomi, M. (2006). Comments on Professors Kraemer and Detrick's paper, "ITCs in intercorporate production networks: Global IT and local *guanxi* in the PC industry." Mimeo. Tokyo: Research Institute of Economy, Trade, and Industry.

Yoshitomi, M. & Ohno, K. (1999). Capital-account crisis and credit contraction. ADBI Working Paper No. 2. Tokyo: Asian Development Bank Institute.

# Acknowledgments

I thank Professor Kenneth Reinert and two anonymous referees for excellent comments. This research is supported by the JSPS Grants-in-Aid for Scientific Research (B, 17H02532). Any errors are my own responsibility.

Cambridge Elements ᵉ

# International Economics

## Kenneth A. Reinert
*George Mason University*
Kenneth A. Reinert is Professor of Public Policy in the Schar School of Policy and Government at George Mason University where he directs the Global Commerce and Policy master's degree program. He is author of *An Introduction to International Economics: New Perspectives on the World Economy* with Cambridge University Press and coauthor of *Globalization for Development: Meeting New Challenges* with Oxford University Press. He is also editor of *The Handbook of Globalisation and Development* with Edward Elgar and co-editor of the two-volume *Princeton Encyclopedia of the World Economy* with Princeton University Press.

## About the Series
International economics is a distinct field with both fundamental theoretical insights and increasing empirical and policy relevance. The *Cambridge Elements in International Economics* series showcases this field, covering the subfields of international trade, international money and finance, and international production, and featuring both established researchers and new contributors from all parts of the world. It aims for a level of theoretical discourse slightly above that of the *Journal of Economic Perspectives* to maintain accessibility. It extends Cambridge University Press' established reputation in international economics into the new, digital format of *Cambridge Elements*. It attempts to fill the niche once occupied by the *Princeton Essays in International Finance*, a series that no longer exists.

There is a great deal of important work that takes place in international economics that is set out in highly theoretical and mathematical terms. This new Elements series does not eschew this work but seeks a broader audience that includes academic economists and researchers, including those working in international organizations such as the World Bank, the International Monetary Fund, and the Organisation for Economic Co-operation and Development.

Cambridge Elements $\equiv$

# International Economics

## Elements in the Series

*Debt Sustainability: A Global Challenge*
Ludger Schuknecht

*Export Quality and Income Distribution*
Rajat Acharyya & Shrimoyee Ganguly

*The East Asian Electronics Industry: The Roles of Exchange Rates, Technology Transfer, and Global Value Chains*
Willem Thorbecke

A full series listing is available at: www.cambridge.org/CEIE

Printed in the United States
by Baker & Taylor Publisher Services